The First-Time Mom's Guide to Raising Boys

The First-Time Mom's Guide to Raising Boys

Practical Advice for Your Son's Formative Years

JENNIFER L. W. FINK

ROCKRIDGE
PRESS

For Nathan, Tyler, Adam, and Sam— you taught me everything I know.

Interior and Cover Designer: Brieanna Felschow
Art Producer: Sara Feinstein
Editor: Mo Mozuch
Production Editor: Sigi Nacson
Production Manager: Jose Olivera

Photography used under license from Shutterstock.com. Author photo courtesy of Red Wolf Photography.

ISBN: 978-1-64876-645-9
eBook 978-1-64876-147-8

R0

Contents

Introduction

"How do you do it?"

I looked up, surprised. Was the always-calm-and-smiling-mother-of-10-children really asking *me* how I manage? At the time, I had three young sons and often felt like I was floundering. By contrast, the mom talking to me always seemed in control. And her kids were well-behaved!

As our conversation continued, the subtext of her question became clear: What she really wanted to know was how to effectively parent *boys*. Her first seven children were all girls; number eight was a boy who was not responding to the techniques she used with her girls.

That encounter was the first time I realized that parenting boys requires a unique skill set—an understanding of male development, coupled with knowledge of "boy culture" and a tolerance for chaos. When my fourth son was born, I began telling people that I "specialized" in boys.

My oldest son turned 9 that same year, and I soon realized how little I knew. I didn't know then that my oldest was likely starting puberty. I didn't know how to handle his intensity. My son's moods infected our house, and when he didn't do what he was supposed to, I was at a loss. How *does* one discipline a child who is completely determined, tech savvy, and almost as big as you are?

I spent most of the next few years feeling absolutely overwhelmed. I cried. I journaled. I muddled through.

I survived, though, and so did my son. In fact, by the time he hit his late teens, it was as if a switch had flipped. The moody and mercurial boy was gone; in his place stood a young man who was kind, decent, and funny.

I realized that I'd spent six years or so trying to *find the answer*—trying to fix what was wrong with my son—when, in reality, nothing was wrong. He was growing, plain and simple.

His mind and body, and our relationship, were just changing. He was going through a completely normal and natural
stage, a stage that starts (for boys) around age 10, give or take a
few years.

This book explores that stage. In Part One, we'll discuss the
emotional, social, cognitive, physical, and sexual changes your
son will experience over the next few years. I'll also encourage
you to think deeply about your parenting and your own past.
The tween years (approximately ages 8 to 12) call for deliberate,
thoughtful parenting; the strategies that worked when your son
was younger need to be adapted, and upgrading your parenting
toolbox may require you to unpack some experiences from your
own childhood. There are also anecdotes throughout to illustrate
that you are not alone in dealing with any of this.

Part Two walks you through how to support your son
during this period of transition. I'll share concrete strategies
you can use to address educational challenges, social dilemmas,
bullying, digital distractions, and mental health concerns, as well
as scripts you can use to discuss dating and consent.

Your son's world is expanding, so in Part Three, we tackle
the larger issues that affect our families and communities: addiction and substance use disorder, violence, illness and death,
racism, sexism, inequity, and natural disasters. At first glance,
these topics may seem out of place in a parenting book, but we
have to help our sons make sense of the world they're living in.
We can't shy away from the tough topics.

My boys are now teenagers and young adults. We regularly
discuss and debate current events, and my sons are the first
to remind me that I don't know everything about raising boys.
They're right: I've never been a boy and I *don't* know what it's
like to be a boy today. I've learned a lot, though, and I've poured
every bit of that knowledge into this book.

My sons have grown into incredible human beings, despite
my mistakes, missteps, and fears. Your son can, too.

Special Note to First-Time Moms

Your first trip through the tween years can be a bit terrifying! Your son is growing and changing, and, honestly, you're not sure you're even up to the task of guiding your gangly, goofy son to manhood. (Somehow, most of us never really consider this stage when we first become parents.)

The fear, hesitation, and doubt you're feeling right now are completely normal. In fact, those emotions are a sign that you're a great mom. You care deeply about your son and you want to do right by him. You're determined to raise a good guy.

A word of advice: Don't forget to have fun. Seize small moments of joy. Laugh with your son at farts and bathroom jokes. Wrestle with him, while you still can. Try to say yes more often than you say no; there's really nothing wrong with cookies for breakfast or a later-than-usual bedtime so that you can enjoy a movie together.

You might want to keep a pen nearby as you read this book. Feel free to jot your thoughts and observations in the margins. Someday, those notes will make you smile.

PART ONE

A Time of Growth for Mother and Son

Wondering what happened to your little boy? You're not alone. Many moms are blindsided by their sons' sudden desire to spend more time alone—and confused when the boy who once enjoyed cuddling begins shrinking away from physical affection.

Your son is entering a whole new period of growth. He's changing physically and mentally, and your relationship has to change, too. It's time for you to learn how to support your son as he grows toward independence.

Growth can be painful at times, but when you understand what's happening with your son, you'll be better equipped to respond with love.

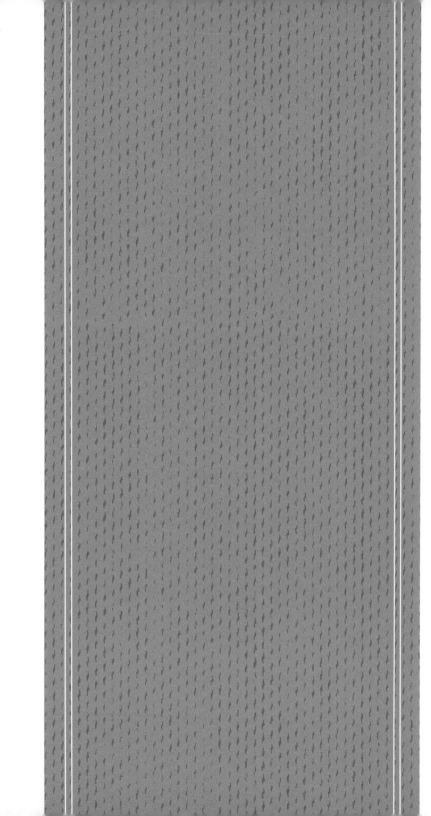

CHAPTER ONE

A Changing Mind and Body

BIG changes are headed your family's way.

Boys' minds and bodies change a lot between ages 8 and 12. You'll see your sweet son grow into an independent boy who likes to do things his own way. His friends may become more important than his family, but his increasing need for independence doesn't mean that he doesn't love or need you. He's moving into a new phase of life—which means you are, too.

Understanding the coming changes will help you adapt your parenting to meet your son's evolving needs.

Emotional Development

Think of all the emotions your son has already experienced: Love. Joy. Anger. Fear. Sadness.

He's developed a basic emotional vocabulary and understanding of human relationships. Over the next few years, his knowledge of emotions and relationships will explode—and, like all explosions, this one won't be neat. Emotional development may be chaotic and messy.

Before age 8, most children are relatively unaware of others. They know other humans exist, of course, but only in relation to them. You're simply "Mom" to a young boy, a person who cares for him and feeds him; young children don't recognize their parents or others as complex human beings.

Around age 9, though, children experience what Waldorf educators call the "nine-year change." They become increasingly aware that they are separate, independent beings and they begin to develop a sense of self. Between ages 8 and 12, boys also develop an increased awareness of others. This increased awareness can lead to intense self-consciousness, shame, embarrassment, and low self-esteem, especially if boys don't understand *why* they're experiencing such strong emotions.

Your son—and you—may be surprised by sudden mood swings and conflicting desires. He may be tempted to suppress or hide his emotions, and he'll get plenty of encouragement to do so. For generations, boys and men have been told to stop crying and "man up." And while it may seem preferable, in the moment, for your son to stuff uncomfortable emotions down, he'll be better off in the long run if he learns how to identify and express his feelings.

All boys experience significant emotional development during the tween years. However, each boy grows and matures according to his unique time line.

Balancing complex emotions and interactions

Tween boys can be easily overwhelmed by emotions—in part because they can now experience multiple emotions at once. A boy who fails a test may feel sadness, disappointment, anger, shame, and self-loathing. He's conscious of his own feelings *and* that both you and his teacher may have thoughts and feelings about his performance. That's a lot of emotion to untangle, and boys this age don't yet have the ability to effectively manage all those feelings. So, often, they lash out.

You can help your son develop his emotional intelligence by teaching him to identify and name his emotions. If your son grumbles or storms out of the room when you ask about his test, give him some time to settle down before revisiting the issue. In a calm moment, try saying something like, "I'll bet you felt pretty lousy when you saw your grade on that test." Keep the judgment out of your voice and introduce words like *embarrassment* and *regret* as appropriate.

Egocentrism

It is totally normal for preteen boys to act as if the world revolves around them. In fact, one developmental task of adolescence is to recognize that other people perceive and experience the world differently and that their thoughts and feelings also deserve consideration.

Your son is not there yet. At around age 11, boys develop an acute awareness of others, but only in relation to themselves. They believe that others notice and care deeply about their appearance and behavior, which is one reason boys care about trends. They also believe that their feelings and experiences are unique, which is why stories about your childhood trigger eye rolls. Your son doesn't yet understand that all humans go through this intensely self-conscious stage.

Increased need for privacy

Has your son started spending more time in his room and apart from the family? Around age 10, most boys (and girls) start pulling away. This desire for privacy can be really unsettling, but it's simply a sign that your son is growing up.

Your son needs time alone to process his emotions and pursue his own interests. He's beginning to develop a sense of himself as a separate person, which means that the boy who once eagerly jumped at the chance to go on a bike ride with you may now decline your offers. He probably won't tell you as much about his personal life, either. He might refuse to tell you why he's upset after school or only reluctantly tell you the names of new friends.

Respect your son's newfound need for privacy, but try to find ways to maintain closeness. Family traditions, like a weekly pizza night, can be helpful.

Expanded empathy

Empathy is the ability to understand and feel the emotions of others. It's crucial to healthy relationships.

Your son is increasingly aware of the fact that other people have their own thoughts and feelings, so now is a perfect time to talk about and teach empathy. Traditionally, boys have not been taught to consider the emotions of others, yet research has consistently linked empathy with happiness and success. Children who demonstrate empathy tend to feel good about themselves and do better in school. Long term, they live happier, healthier lives.

Remember: The development of empathy is a process. You will often be frustrated by your son's apparent lack of concern for others. Keep at it. Having adults in your son's life demonstrate empathy is one way to expand his emotional intelligence.

Aggression and mood swings

Believe it or not, the first changes of puberty can begin as early as age 9. Most of these early changes aren't visible to parents—except the mood swings and aggression.

Irritability and outbursts are common in the middle school years. Increased levels of testosterone contribute to an increase in anger and aggression. Increased academic and social pressure plays a role as well.

Another factor: Anger is considered an acceptable emotion for boys and men, while fear and sadness are taboo. That tired stereotype is gradually being replaced with an acknowledgment that all humans should be allowed the full range of emotional expression, but by the time boys reach elementary school, they've already seen countless images of angry males using aggression to solve problems.

Boys need our help to understand their mood swings. They need us to explain the hormonal changes that trigger sudden emotional shifts. Otherwise, it's easy for our boys to think that something is wrong with them.

Boys also need our help to discover productive ways to manage aggression and mood swings. Physical activity almost always helps. Encourage your son to go for a bike ride or a run, or allow him to smash boxes or empty cans.

Shame and embarrassment

Remember how your son used to tear his clothes off and run through the house, no matter who was present? Those days are long gone.

Little kids don't care what other people think about their appearance or behavior. Older kids care *a lot* because they've learned that other people's opinions matter. They're no longer confident that the world will love them simply because they're cute and special.

Because tween boys are acutely aware of others' opinions and reactions, they are prone to shame and embarrassment. Boys now notice when they fall short of others' expectations, and a failure to measure up can unleash profound feelings of disappointment and self-loathing.

Boys are especially vulnerable to shame. When they are berated and humiliated, they're quick to assume they're inherently bad. Shame and embarrassment should never be used as disciplinary tools. Your son needs your love, support, and teaching instead.

Low self-esteem and depression

Boys are constantly searching for the answer to one question: *Am I okay?*

If the messages they receive from other people—via low grades, social ostracism, negative comments—suggest they are not meeting expectations, boys' self-esteem plummets. Some fall into depression.

You can support the development of healthy self-esteem by acknowledging your son's unique skills and talents. Giving him opportunities to solve problems and pursue his interests can also help. Teaching (and modeling) self-care rituals, such as daily exercise and spending time in nature, will help him cope with stress and may stave off depression.

If you're concerned about your son's self-esteem and mental health, talk to his school counselor or health-care provider.

Social Development

Your boy's world is about to get a whole lot bigger.

During the tween years, his focus will shift from his family to his peers. Friendships become primary; social acceptance is everything.

In the early elementary school years, boys typically prefer to play with boys. Around age 8 or 9, many expand their friendship circles to include kids of all genders. They may also develop their first romantic crushes. By age 12, most boys have experienced physical and emotional attraction.

Clubs and teams may play an important role in your son's social development. Athletic boys often find acceptance and belonging on a sports team. Other boys may find camaraderie and friendship at dance school or in a robotics club. Still other boys form friendships through shared interests. Your son's desire for acceptance may make it difficult for him to fully express himself; you may see him suppress parts of his personality or act in uncharacteristic ways as he attempts to fit in.

Shift in relationship priorities

You are no longer number one in your son's life.

Preteens want to spend most of their time with friends, in person and online. (The video games your son plays are one way he stays connected with friends.) Friends expand a boy's understanding of the world and help him understand his role within it.

It may be hard for parents to accept the fact that their son now prefers to spend his time with his peers. But his preference for his friends is not a rejection of you. You remain a strong influence in your son's life—even if he doesn't want to spend much time with you.

Strong sense of independence and power

Between ages 8 and 12, children develop a sense of themselves as powerful, capable humans, if we let them. Unfortunately, many parents unwittingly hamper their boy's development. Our fears and concerns can lead us to hover; we feel more comfortable monitoring his assignments than turning over responsibility to him, lest he fail.

But the preteen years are the perfect time to give your son additional independence. Let him handle conflicts with friends and decide how to spend his money. Put him in charge of his homework. Sure, he'll make some mistakes, but better to make them now while the stakes are relatively low.

Becoming sensitive to what others think of them

We don't often think of tween boys as sensitive creatures, but they are. They are constantly monitoring the metaphoric (and literal) room to see what others think about them. Their increased sensitivity to others' opinions, combined with their desire to fit in, is one reason that peer pressure is so powerful at this age.

You can counteract potentially negative messages from his peers by frequently reminding your son of his positive, unique characteristics.

Expanded prosocial skills

Your son won't always be generous and kind (are any of us?), but you may notice him taking an interest in the world at large. He may ask questions about current events and social justice, and he may express a desire to help make the world a better place. Help him find and connect with volunteer opportunities in your community.

Most of your son's prosocial skills will be directed toward his friends; young boys can be incredibly loving and protective of one another, even though what you see on the surface looks primarily like clowning around.

Strong sense of fairness

Even very young children can tell when something isn't fair. According to research, 1-year-old children expect resources to be divided fairly and preschoolers protest if they receive less than their peers.

This seemingly innate desire for justice kicks into overdrive in the preteen years. Because your son is now more aware of others, he's also aware of unequal treatment. Combine that with his preadolescent egocentrism, and you will almost certainly hear him say something like "She has it in for me!" or "The coach doesn't treat me fairly!"

Listen to your son, but don't automatically jump in and side with him. You may want to connect with his teacher or coach to get the full story.

As your son grows, his understanding of "fair" will expand as well. It takes a long time for children to develop a mature sense of justice.

Cognitive Development

Your son's brain is busy making all kinds of connections. Over the next few years, he'll develop the ability to think abstractly. He'll begin to apply logic and reasoning to his experiences and arguments—which means you'll face an increasingly formidable debate partner. (Most kids' vocabulary increases by an average of 3,000 words per year in late childhood/early adolescence.) Additional neural connections in the brain will allow him to process information more quickly; this amped-up processing power is one reason preteens pick up new skills relatively quickly.

Of course, all kids are different. Boys with attention-deficit/hyperactivity disorder (ADHD), autism spectrum disorder, dyslexia, or other physical and emotional challenges develop at a different trajectory then their peers. Chapter 5 includes strategies you can use to support your son's cognitive development.

Reasoning and logical arguments

Your son will soon be able to tell when something "doesn't make sense." A 10-year-old boy understands that a long row of five pennies is worth just as much as a stack of five pennies; a 5-year-old would struggle with that concept.

Children's ability to apply past learning to current problems helps them tremendously in school and in life. As your son's ability to make logical arguments increases, though, you may notice an increase in "talking back." He doesn't intend to be rude or disrespectful; he's merely testing his cognitive skills. Keep your voice and demeanor calm, and continue to enforce boundaries even as you explain your reasoning.

Identity

Have you seen videos of babies bursting into tears after their dads shave off their mustaches or beards? These infants knew their fathers with facial hair; after the hair was gone, the man in front of them seemed to be a stranger.

Infants and young children don't recognize the difference between inherent and superficial traits. They don't know that the man beneath is the same, regardless of his hair. Older children understand that identity is consistent.

This evolving understanding of identity means that boys can become distressed if they see friends or loved ones behaving in inconsistent ways.

Perspective

During their preteen years, children develop the ability to view things from multiple perspectives. They begin to realize that other people may perceive a situation differently than they do. This increased ability to understand perspective will help your son become a good friend and a good citizen.

You can challenge your son's perspective-taking skills with optical illusions. Casual conversations can also help him unpack other people's reactions to situations and events. It takes a long time for boys to grow into full awareness of others' needs—and you'll likely see many instances of self-centered behavior over the next few years—but his ability to consider other perspectives is growing.

Increased attention abilities

The average 8-year-old can pay attention for 16 to 24 minutes. A 10-year-old has an average attention span of 20 to 30 minutes. By age 12, most children can sustain attention for about half an hour.

Of course, these averages vary greatly, depending on distractions, mood, and physical conditions like hunger and room temperature. And all humans can maintain attention and focus better when they're doing something they enjoy. That's why your Lego-loving son can build his Lego towers for hours, but tire quickly when doing homework.

Note: Contrary to popular belief, boys with ADHD can sustain attention for a long time—*if* they're doing something they enjoy. That's why some boys with ADHD can play video games or build things with empty boxes for hours, but struggle when you ask them to do their math homework.

MILESTONE DEVELOPMENTS AREN'T FIXED

Some babies walk by 9 months. Others crawl and scoot until well after their first birthday. By age 2, almost all typically developing children are walking.

Variations in development are completely natural and normal. These differences can be really distressing to tween boys, though, as they're constantly trying to measure up to their peers.

Remind your son (and yourself, as needed) that people develop according to their own unique timetables. Pointing out some general variations in development can help, too.

Did you know, for instance, that the parts of the brain that handle language and impulse control mature, on average, sooner in girls than in boys? Sharing these facts with your son may help him understand why girls in his class tend to succeed while he and his friends are getting in trouble and falling behind, despite their best efforts.

Physical and Sexual Development

Boys begin puberty, on average, around age 11 or 12. However, some boys start puberty as early as 8 years old.

The first signs of puberty are often invisible to parents. As Dr. Cara Natterson writes in her book *Decoding Boys*, "early puberty is essentially invisible to the outside world because the only measurable changes are happening inside their testicles."

What you may notice: Mood swings. Irritability. Subtle changes to your son's face. Soon, he'll look less like a little boy and more like, well, a big kid.

Because boys, like girls, hit puberty at different ages, those who are ahead or behind the curve may feel really self-conscious. Boys who mature late often struggle because they feel they can't compete, physically or otherwise, with same-age peers who've already hit growth spurts and show signs of maturity. They are more likely to experience low self-esteem, have fewer friends than boys who develop early, and tend to do worse in school. According to Dr. Natterson, 2.5 out of every 100 boys is a "late bloomer."

There's not much you or your son can do to speed up (or slow down) his growth. You can, however, make sure he understands the changes headed his way. If he's a late bloomer, pay special attention to his emotional needs. He may feel self-conscious or anxious, wondering if puberty will *ever* start or if he'll ever attract romantic attention. Empathize with your son ("Yeah, it stinks to be the last one to hit a growth spurt"), remind him of his special attributes ("You manage to make me laugh like no one else"), and share any family stories that might ease his mind ("Uncle Greg was the smallest kid on his seventh grade basketball team, too. Now he's over six feet tall!"). Ask his father, or another male role model, to share stories of how they experienced changes growing up as well.

Hormonal changes and the role of testosterone

Testosterone is often called a male hormone, but that's not entirely accurate.

All humans have testosterone in their systems; however, teenage and adult males generally have much higher levels than females.

In early puberty, the pituitary gland (which is located at the base of the brain) secretes two hormones that tell the testes to ramp up production of testosterone. Meanwhile, the sensitivity to testosterone is reset in boys' brains at this time.

Over the next years, testosterone will reshape your son's body.

Physical changes

Testosterone triggers growth of the penis and testicles. Testosterone also sparks growth spurts, increases in lean body mass, voice changes, and the growth of facial hair.

Boys' voices typically begin changing between the ages of 11 and 16, so you can expect some voice cracking over the next few years. Many boys have fun with their changing voices, but some are embarrassed by their unpredictable sound. Vocal changes can be especially tough for boys who sing.

Facial hair doesn't usually appear until around age 15, but some boys have obvious mustaches at age 12 or 13.

Sexual changes

Puberty is the process of sexual maturity. As your son moves through puberty, his interest in sex will grow. He'll also develop the physical capacity to father children.

Most boys experience their first nocturnal emission ("wet dream")—an emission of semen during sleep—between ages 9 and 15. Wet dreams are completely normal, but if a boy doesn't know anything about them, he may assume that he wet the bed. Talk to your son about the physical changes of puberty before age 9 (and frequently afterward) so that he knows what to expect. Nocturnal emissions are more common among boys who sleep on their stomachs, so if your son is having them frequently, consider suggesting an adjustment in his sleep position.

FOR YOUR REFLECTION

1. Which changes are you looking forward to?
2. What scares you the most about the upcoming changes in your son's life?
3. How do you plan to support your son's emotional development?
4. How much do you know about male puberty? Where will you go to get more information?

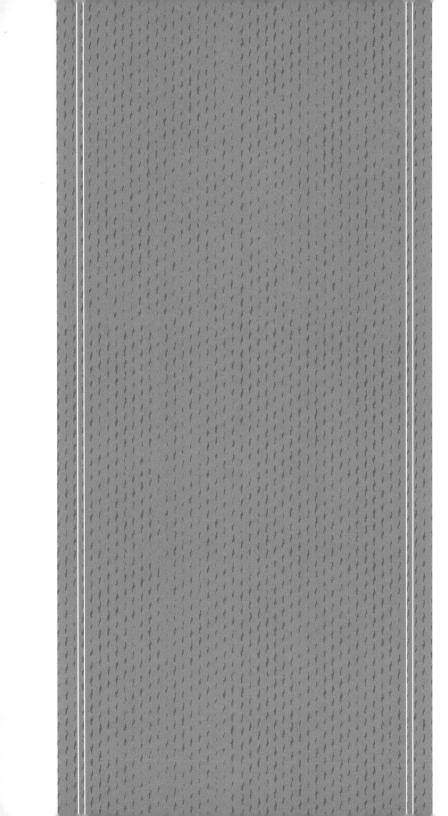

CHAPTER TWO

For Mom: Determining Parenting Goals and Defining Your Values

Raising boys isn't easy.

You already know this fact, of course. But as your boy moves out of childhood and into early adolescence, your parenting relationship must shift. He won't need you to *do* things for him much anymore; instead, he'll need you to provide scaffolding and support so that he can act on his own. You may find it difficult to give your son more control over his life, but allowing kids to take risks helps them develop persistence, grit, and confidence.

Now is a great time to think carefully about how you'll parent your son over the next few years. Do you want to parent him as you or his other parent were raised, or do you want to try a different approach? Defining your values will help you respond effectively and intentionally to your son's behavior.

Envisioning Your Goals and Building a Support Network

Close your eyes and picture your son moving through the world as a full-grown adult. What's he like? How does he treat other people?

How you describe your idealized-and-imagined adult son can tell you a lot about what's important to you. If you envisioned a man who is kind, competent, and self-supporting, you likely value kindness, compassion, self-motivation, and independence. You can take steps now to increase the likelihood that your vision will become a reality.

Effective parenting depends, in part, on clearly defined goals. What exactly are you trying to accomplish? Do you want your son to unquestioningly do everything he's told, or do you want him to critically evaluate information and make choices that align with his values?

As your son approaches his teenage years, it's vitally important for you to identify your end goals. Think carefully about, and even jot down, what "success" and "happiness" mean to you. If you have a partner, ask them to do this exercise as well. Then discuss your thoughts with your son; he may surprise you with profound insights. (Or not. Don't get your hopes up!)

Remember: Your son is a unique human being and so are you. There is no one "right way" to raise a boy. Together, you'll forge a path that suits both of you.

Dealing with first-time mom nerves

You've never parented a tween boy before. No wonder you don't know what you're doing.

All parents feel nervous and unsure when their children enter a new stage of life. You know the stakes are about to get higher and, on some level, you know the parenting tricks you've mastered won't work with a preteen.

As a woman, you're also acutely aware of the importance of raising good men. You've probably encountered plenty of narcissistic men and sexist jerks, and you don't want to unleash another one on the world.

So, you're trying to figure out how to raise a gentleman—while your son farts his way through dinner.

Breathe. Your anxiety is completely normal. You care deeply for your son, and that will pull you through the next few years. You'll make mistakes; we all do. But your love will drive you to reflect, learn from others, and seek information and support.

Uncertainty and anxiety are part of parenting. Tilt the odds in your favor by building a strong support system and learning all you can about boys.

Finding your community

Boy moms need other boy moms.

You can learn lots of useful parenting tips from grandparents, teachers, experts, and moms of girls, but boy moms are the ones who understand the chaos and confusion that is your household. Boy moms will tell you about the calls they've also received from school, and they will not judge you if your son decides to add a penis to the snowman in front of your house.

Without input from other parents of boys, it's easy to conclude that your parenting, or your son, is bad. Only when you connect with other moms of boys do you realize that many—if not most—families are dealing with similar issues.

Boy moms will be your best source of support and information. They can share tried-and-true parenting strategies that will help you survive your son's preteen years and adolescence.

Strike up conversation on the sidelines.

If your son plays a sport, chat up the other moms in the stands. Introduce yourself, point out your son, and ask about their sons. Share the truth of your experience—stinky soccer cleats in the car—to encourage them to speak honestly as well.

Go online.

Facebook has all kinds of groups for parents of boys, including Building Boys, Boymom Squad, and Moms of Boys. Use the hashtags #boymom and #momofboys to find other boy moms on Instagram and Twitter. You'll meet moms from all over the world—and discover that parents worldwide are struggling with the same issues you are.

Cultivate friendships with moms who mention their boys.

If a work colleague or a casual acquaintance shares a story about her son, make it a point to connect with her later. Comment on her story and tell her about your son; the fact that you're both parenting boys means you're likely to have something in common.

Unlearn Parenting

You didn't have a perfect childhood. Likely, your parents did some things right and some things that, well, really hurt you.

Now is the time to carefully examine your childhood because if you don't, you'll probably repeat your parents' mistakes. Despite our best intentions, most of us parent as our parents did, simply because that's what we know. But our parents' parenting was influenced by *their* parents, as well as their social, cultural, and economic status. The discipline strategies your parents used in the '80s and '90s may have been based on 1950s child-rearing advice—which might not be particularly useful in raising a 21st-century kid.

Think about your parents' disciplinary techniques. Would you say they were effective, or not? Did you change your behavior because of your parents' actions or did you simply hide your misdeeds? When you encountered a problem, did you go to your parents for help, or did you avoid them because you were afraid of their reactions?

It may be uncomfortable to think critically about your childhood, but an honest accounting can help you decide which parenting practices you want to keep and which you want to "unlearn," or discard.

Letting go of control

When your son is young, you control nearly every aspect of his daily life: what clothes he wears, when and what he eats, when he sleeps, and where he goes. As he gets older, you must gradually release control.

That's easier said than done. It's one thing to let him pick out his own clothes, and another to allow him to walk or bike to school alone.

Giving your child freedom and space to make decisions (and mistakes) is terrifying. It's also absolutely necessary. Boys who do not have autonomy over their lives grow into adults who are paralyzed by indecision and low self-esteem, while boys who've learned to recalibrate after mistakes navigate adulthood with confidence.

Parents' well-intentioned desire to keep their children safe can limit their sons' growth. It's not yet time to turn over the reins completely, but your son needs space to take some physical and emotional risks. When he asks to do something new, stop and think before you respond. Don't allow fear to control your response.

When you're struggling to release control, ask yourself, *Do I want to be a mother who limits my son or one who facilitates his growth?*

Addressing Your Own Childhood

Why are we devoting so much time to your childhood? Because your childhood experiences shaped your beliefs about family and yourself. Identifying and resolving lingering issues will allow you to parent your son from a position of strength.

If your family avoided conflict, you may not know how to have a healthy disagreement. You might find yourself getting anxious or angry when your son expresses an opposing opinion. If, as a child, you were expected to obey your parents without question, you might snap at your son when he asks why has to do the dishes.

We all carry with us hurt, pain, and unresolved issues from childhood. Most adults, though, devote more time and energy to suppressing their pain than addressing it. That approach may work for a while, but it probably won't hold up under stress.

Negative self-talk, conflict avoidance, difficulty finding and feeling joy, or even consistently putting other people's priorities ahead of your own when doing so causes you harm can be symptoms of unresolved childhood issues.

If you have a hard time trusting others or establishing boundaries, you may benefit from professional assistance. A therapist or counselor can help you work through the emotional pain of your childhood and establish healthy coping mechanisms. Parenting coaches may help you identify dysfunctional family patterns and choose more effective strategies.

It's not easy to uncover and address childhood pain. After all, most of us learned early on to ignore whatever dysfunction was present in our households. It takes strength, bravery, and maturity to examine our past and tease apart the healthy from the unhealthy. Your love for your son may be the motivation you need to move forward.

Remember: Proactively addressing these issues now will give you a better chance of responding peacefully and productively to preteen and teenage challenges.

Codependency

According to the nonprofit organization Mental Health America, codependency is a learned behavior that is often passed down from generation to generation. A codependent relationship is one that is one-sided and emotionally destructive or abusive.

People who are codependent spend the bulk of their time trying to fix others' problems. The codependent child or spouse of an alcoholic, for instance, may hide evidence of drinking binges, clean up vomit, and tuck the alcoholic into bed, even if doing so means neglecting their own work. They deny or ignore their pain, anger, and frustration, and attempt to derive self-worth from caregiving. Unfortunately, the codependent's efforts make it easier for their loved one to continue self-destructive behavior and more difficult for the codependent to develop an independent identity.

Codependency can lead to low self-esteem and a tendency to focus on the needs of others. If you are prone to codependent behavior, your default setting may be to focus all your time and attention on your son. Your natural inclination may be to "clean up" his mistakes, but protecting him from consequences can hinder his development.

The book *Codependent No More*, by Melody Beattie, is a great resource. A good therapist can also help you maintain healthy boundaries.

Addiction problems

If you grew up with a parent who was addicted to alcohol or drugs, your childhood may have been marked by instability. Sometimes your parents were loving and kind. At other times, they were terrifying and unreliable. At a young age, you may have had to assume responsibility for yourself and others.

Living with a sibling with a substance use disorder can be traumatic as well and affect you long after you leave home.

It may be difficult to acknowledge the impact of substance use, but admitting the reality of your experience and seeking counseling can help you avoid repeating unhealthy patterns.

Al-Anon groups support people who have been affected by others' drinking or drug use; you can go to their website to find a group near you. Nar-Anon offers similar 12-step groups designed for friends and families of addicts.

Note: If one of your biological relatives has (or had) a substance use disorder, you and your son may be prone to addiction as well. If you are worried about your drinking or drug use, consult your physician or primary care provider. Groups like Alcoholics Anonymous (AA) and Narcotics Anonymous (NA) can also be helpful.

Parentification

Parents are supposed to care for and protect their children. If a parent is unable or unwilling to do so, roles may be reversed: The child may end up providing physical and emotional support for the parent.

Psychologists define *parentification* as "a family process involving developmentally inappropriate expectations that children function in a parental role within stressed, disorganized family systems." If you were regularly expected to cook dinner, grocery shop, or care for younger siblings, you may have experienced parentification. Children who serve as their parents' emotional confidants may also be victims of parentification.

Having such confidence and trust placed in you at a young age can make it difficult to define appropriate boundaries and expectations. After all, if you were expected to prepare dinner every night at age 10, why shouldn't your son cook for the family? And if your mom always told you about problems with your father, it might seem perfectly natural for you to confide in your son as well.

However, parentification hinders child development. A child who is focused on the parent neglects their own needs—and has little to no practice relying on others. A good therapist can help you heal and establish a more appropriate relationship with your child.

Mental illness

According to the UK's Royal College of Psychiatrists, more than two-thirds of women and half of men with mental health problems are parents. If your mother or father (or a sibling) has anxiety, depression, obsessive-compulsive disorder, bipolar disorder, or post-traumatic stress disorder (PTSD), your childhood may have included neglect or erratic behavior. You likely coped as best you could, which may lead to lifelong tendencies toward hypervigilance, perfectionism, and distrust.

Because mental illness runs in families—a combination of genetics and environment—it's possible that you may also have anxiety, depression, or another mental health disorder. Seeking treatment may help you be a happier, healthier parent, and may minimize the chances that your child will also develop mental illness. You cannot change your genetic inheritance, but you can take steps today toward better mental health. Those steps may change the trajectory of your family's future.

Taking Care of Yourself

You cannot effectively parent your son while you're in a state of stress yourself. Despite your best efforts and carefully chosen words, your son will sense and respond to your anger, fear, frustration, and concern. Taking time for yourself—both in moments of high stress and on a regular basis—allows you to parent from a place of peace, which, in turn, allows your son's nervous system to relax.

Most moms struggle with the concept of self-care because there's simply *so much to do*. How in the world are we supposed to carve out time for ourselves when the day is already too short? But here's the thing: Self-care makes everything easier. When we give ourselves time to de-stress, we don't spend as much time spinning our proverbial wheels or arguing with our sons. Self-care allows us to operate from a position of strength, not weakness. Consider time for yourself an investment in your health, well-being, and parenting.

Get moving

Physical activity releases feel-good brain chemicals, and who doesn't need more of those? You don't have to embark on an ambitious exercise program to benefit, either. A simple walk around the block can raise your heart rate and clear your mind; so can playing catch or basketball with your son.

Aim for 30 minutes of movement every day, but don't fret if you sometimes miss your goal. Even 5 minutes of physical activity is better than none.

Commune with nature

It's generally understood that humans need time in nature for optimal physical, mental, and spiritual health. Exposure to sunshine and natural light releases serotonin (a feel-good brain chemical), decreases blood pressure, and improves sleep. Observing animals—even through a city window—can also decrease blood pressure, heart rate, and anxiety.

Whenever possible, try to combine physical activity and time in nature. Garden on your back porch or go for a walk at a city or state park.

Write it out

Author and creativity expert Julia Cameron advises people to write three pages by hand each morning. (If three sounds like a lot, start with one.) This practice, which Cameron has dubbed "Morning Pages," is a form of journaling. You simply write whatever pops into your head, stream of consciousness–style. (Yes, that may mean writing *I don't know what to write* five times before something else comes to mind.)

Journaling can help you process your emotions and solve problems. Your notebook or journal is a safe place to vent and dream. You can experiment until you find a form of journaling that feels right to you. Some people sketch, paint, or create collages in their journals in lieu of writing.

Define and Model Your Values

By age 8, most boys are pros at tuning out their moms. They can spot an incoming lecture and dodge the conversation before you make a single point. It is crucially important to keep the lines of communication open, but we can't rely on verbal lessons alone—especially with boys, who tend to be tactile, experiential learners.

That's why role-modeling is the most effective parenting tool of all.

According to a Harvard survey, about 80 percent of surveyed young students believe their parents are more concerned about achievement and personal happiness than caring for others. Why? Because kids hear us harping about homework and grades and see us striving for prestige and status.

If you want to raise a man of character, it's imperative that you clearly define and model your values.

Respect

Is respect earned or inherent?

According to one definition, *respect* is "a feeling of deep admiration for someone elicited by their abilities, qualities, or achievements." That kind of respect is earned.

Another definition states that *respect* is "a sense of the worth of a person." Thus, all humans are worthy of respect.

Pondering the meaning of *respect* is important because your meaning must be clear when you tell your son to "respect others." Do you believe that all people should be treated civilly and accorded basic courtesies? If so, you must explicitly describe for your son what that entails. ("Look in a person's eyes when you greet them," "Follow your teacher's instructions the first time she asks.") If you believe respect is earned via achievement, how would you like your son to demonstrate respect for veterans, for instance? What about grocery store workers? How should he treat people experiencing homelessness?

Trust

According to the Boy Scouts of America, a person who is trustworthy is honest and dependable; they act with integrity and live up to their word. And, yes, that's a lot easier to say than it is to live; the Boy Scouts have certainly fallen short of the mark in the past.

Your son will violate your trust in the coming years. He'll tell you he's done his homework when he hasn't because he wants to play video games. Right now, it's up to you to role-model honesty and dependability. Don't make promises you can't keep—and avoid platitudes. Let your son know that your trust in him will grow as he demonstrates responsibility.

Honesty and openness

By now, your son knows the difference between the truth and a lie. Telling the whole truth, as opposed to leaving a few key details out—well, that's another thing.

Tween boys' increased need for privacy means they're not as likely to speak openly with you. You can dramatically increase the chances of your son coming to you and speaking honestly when needed if you control your emotional reaction when he tells you something tough or disappointing. If you freak out when he tells you he got a D on a test, he probably won't tell you about nude pics he's seen online.

Kindness and sensitivity

Kindness is marked by generosity, consideration, and concern for others. It's intimately linked with sensitivity because when you can sense another person's needs, you can respond with appropriate kindness.

One of the most loving things you can do for your son is show him kindness when he makes a mistake. Australian author and "boy champion" Maggie Dent often made a hot, soothing drink for her sons after an argument; she dropped the drink off at their room without saying another word.

Dent says it is important to model kindness while children are "walking the bridge to adulthood" as "they cannot be what they haven't seen or experienced."

Empathy and compassion

Empathy is the ability to feel what someone else is feeling. It drives compassion because when you can feel the pain and suffering of another, you're moved to relieve their discomfort.

Humans are hardwired for empathy, but it takes time to develop. You can help your son develop empathy by asking him to imagine how he'd feel if he were bullied, excluded, or unfairly profiled.

Integrity

One thing your son will soon realize: A lot of people don't live a life of integrity. Our world is filled with dishonest people who violate moral and ethical principles—some very "successful" in terms of money and power.

You'll have to help your son grapple with that realization. He'll want to know why he should live a moral life when others don't and are rewarded. It will be your job to defend integrity and show him the benefits of a life well-lived. Surround your son with as many people of integrity as possible.

Responsibility

Boys want to make a difference in the world. They don't want to empty the dishwasher, take out the trash, or clean their room.

Your son can (and should) begin taking on additional responsibilities, but you'll have the best luck if you consider his interests, talents, and input in assigning responsibilities. Got a budding chef? Put him in charge of cooking one meal a week. A budding mechanic can help with home and vehicle repairs.

Gratitude

Feeling and expressing thanks is associated with increased happiness and improved mental health, according to numerous studies.

Gratitude is also an antidote to entitlement, as it encourages you to focus on all the good things in your life.

One way to teach your son gratitude is to express your thanks for his help around the house. Yes, picking up his socks is his responsibility, but thanking him provides the positive reinforcement he needs to do it again—and may inspire him to appreciate all the work you do.

Humility

Humility is the opposite of arrogance. An arrogant person believes they are better than others and expects preferential treatment, while a humble person understands that they are no more (or less) important than anyone else.

Preteen boys are not predisposed to humility. The male social hierarchy depends on status, so boys jockey for position—which means you may hear your son bragging about his achievements. Don't call him out in front of his friends; instead, talk with him later.

You can model humility by listening to and considering others' opinions, including your son's.

Inclusivity and diversity

You want your son to welcome, include, and appreciate all people. That's a tall order for a preteen who's concerned about his social standing.

Begin by noticing your own actions. How do you interact with people of different genders, races, cultures, and socioeconomic status? Role-modeling inclusivity and an appreciation of diversity will go a long way.

Don't shy away from tough conversations about race and social justice. The online library of the Center for Racial Justice in Education has lots of resources you can use to educate yourself and stimulate conversation.

It was well after 9 p.m. when I realized that the "swooshing" sound I heard upstairs was not my 9-year-old son rummaging through his Legos, as I'd assumed. The sound was a side effect of my 3-year-old's artistic efforts. He'd scribbled blue crayon all over the walls of our hallway.

It had already been a long day. Somehow, I managed not to scream. After confirming that the crayon was gone ("in the garbage!" he told me), I led my son back to bed, tucked him in (again), and mentally reorganized my to-do list. There was no way I'd get to those walls before midnight.

I went back downstairs and tackled the supper dishes. Again, I heard a strange "swooshing" sound. I hurried upstairs—and found my 11-year-old son scrubbing the crayon off the walls.

From his bedroom, he'd sensed my frustration and exhaustion. And so, my eldest put down the book he was reading and started scrubbing. I was overwhelmed by his empathy, kindness, and compassion.

I told him how much I appreciated his efforts. I thanked him and said he didn't have to continue. He kept working anyway.

"It's easier when it's fresh," he told me. "And blue is one of the easiest colors to get off. Red and black are the hardest." Impressed by his knowledge, I asked him "How do you know?"

He smiled. "Don't look in the back of my closet."

The First-Time Mom's Guide to Raising Boys

10 WAYS TO DEMONSTRATE TRUST

1. Don't check his homework.
2. Ask him to handle an important household task.
3. Let him use real tools.
4. Say "yes" to a risky activity request.
5. Let him handle his own money.
6. Don't nag him.
7. Listen to his side of the story, rather than immediately reacting.
8. Keep his secrets.
9. Follow through on promises.
10. Give him more control over his time and schedule.

FOR YOUR REFLECTION

1. What's your top parenting goal?
2. How will you connect with other "boy moms"?
3. What parenting technique do you want to "unlearn"?
4. How will you care for yourself today? Tomorrow? Next week?
5. What values do you most want to instill in your son?

PART TWO

Between You and Your Son

You and your son have always had a special bond. Your relationship will change over the next few years, but his need for your love and nurturing will not. He'll need your guidance to negotiate the emotional, social, cognitive, and physical changes ahead.

These next chapters will help you teach your son the coping skills he'll need to handle the challenges of middle school (and beyond). You'll learn how to discuss puberty, romance, and sexuality so that your son is prepared to respectfully navigate relationships.

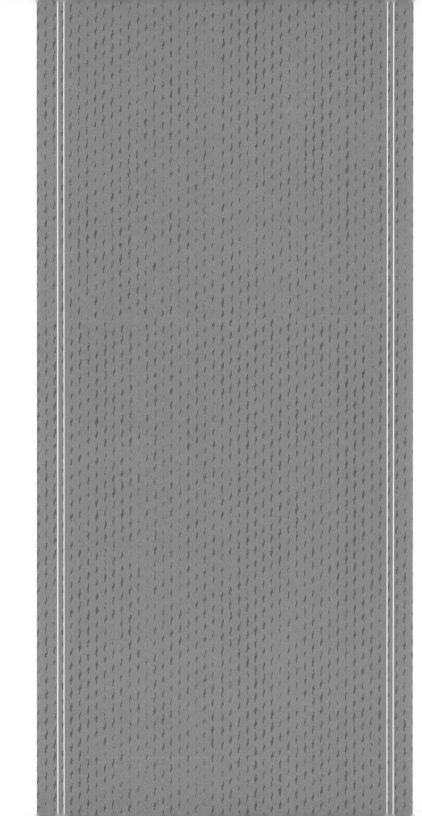

CHAPTER THREE

Caring for Emotional and Mental Health

Your son's mental health matters more than his grades and athletic or extracurricular achievements.

While obvious, this fact has not yet become foundational in parenting or educating boys. We live in a society that glamorizes achievement while glossing over emotions, so parents and teachers alike tend to focus their efforts on developing children's academic, athletic, or artistic acumen. Until very recently, mental health was an afterthought.

Increasingly, though, it has become apparent that it's foolish to ignore boys' emotional well-being. Suicide rates are climbing and boys who don't develop healthy coping skills are more likely to abuse substances and engage in toxic behavior.

This chapter will equip you with tools you can use to build your son's capacity for recognizing, honoring, and expressing emotions.

Building Emotional Intelligence

Emotional intelligence is the ability to identify and respond to emotions (both yours and others') in healthy, productive ways. According to a 2015 article by psychologist Paula Durlofsky, people who have high levels of emotional intelligence experience less anxiety, stress, and unproductive conflict. They're also more likely to experience satisfying relationships.

By contrast, emotional suppression is associated with an increased risk of depression, anxiety, and suicide. The male suicide rate is nearly four times that of females, and experts believe that males' lack of coping skills is one reason for such high levels of lethal self-harm. As science journalist Stephanie Pappas wrote in an article for the American Psychological Association's *Monitor on Psychology*, "Forty years of research [shows] that . . . socializing boys to suppress their emotions causes damage that echoes both inwardly and outwardly."

Naming and understanding emotions

Ian Thomas, a former elementary school teacher, wrote in a 2016 Building Boys blog post that he had noticed that most boys lack adequate vocabulary to describe their emotions.

His male students typically used just three "feeling words": happy, sad, and angry. But just as there's a significant difference between baby blue and midnight blue, there's a chasm between *annoyed* and *irate*—and a boy who lumps both under "angry" is less able to effectively respond to his emotions.

"Being able to accurately identify a feeling and name it with an appropriate word can be extremely helpful in managing the feeling, processing it, accepting it, and moving on," Thomas wrote.

You can teach your son emotions the same way you once taught him colors: Point them out and name them. Except this time, instead of saying "red" when a fire truck drives by, you might say something like the following when you see a man screaming: "Wow! That guy seems *really* angry! He's irate."

Because boys are tactile learners, having a 3-D resource can be helpful, Thomas says. He created Mooshuns—soft, handmade "moody cushions," featuring a variety of facial expressions, available on Etsy—to help children learn to differentiate among their emotions.

Another tactile tool is called Kimochis Mixed Bag of Feelings, which contains a variety of small "feeling pillows" (left out, silly, frustrated, cranky, hopeful, etc.). Put the "feelings" in a central location and periodically grab one that best represents your emotional state and toss it at your son. He'll likely follow suit.

How to manage difficult emotions

None of us are born knowing how to deal with difficult emotions. Toddlers have frequent meltdowns because they don't know what to do with the strong feelings that accompany anger or frustration. You've already taught your son some useful coping skills; now, it's time to teach a few new techniques.

Begin by sharing your own coping mechanisms. How do you get through the tough or stressful parts of your day?

Parents usually handle their emotions in silence. You might step out of the room for a moment when a wave of anger hits or hide in the bathroom when your kids' bickering puts you on edge. These coping skills are largely invisible to your son unless you draw his attention to them. Whenever possible, narrate your emotional process.

You don't need to be a perfect person to teach your son how to handle difficult emotions. When you lose it, verbally revisit the situation later: "I'm so sorry I yelled at you. I was stressed out from work and when you knocked over your milk with your light saber, I overreacted. I should have paused and taken a few deep breaths first."

Mason had always been an intense kid, but things got worse right around his ninth birthday. He worried, a lot.

"He'd lie awake at night thinking about what could happen or go wrong," says Sara, his mom. As a competitive swimmer, Mason was used to having his performance compared to others'. When he was younger, he seemed content in his own skin. At 9, he seemed perpetually unsettled. Nothing he did seemed quite good enough.

Mason's sense of disappointment and shame spiraled into suicidal comments. His parents reached out for help.

"We ended up in therapy with him, and the therapist helped him develop some techniques for handling his anxiety," Sara recalls. After six months, Mason was comfortable enough to discontinue regular therapy.

His parents continue to support his development. "We have to remind him that he did not come pre-loaded with the knowledge of everything at birth," Sara says. "We show and tell him that it's okay to have to learn new things."

Practicing Active Listening

You can help your son learn to differentiate emotions by creating time and space for feelings. That's not as difficult as it might sound—although it may seem challenging and unnatural at first because many of us were raised in households that did not acknowledge feelings or encourage emotional expression.

Active listening is a communication tool that makes space for emotions and helps people truly connect.

There are four steps to active listening:

1. Give your full attention to your child.
2. Make eye contact and stop other things you're doing.
3. Get on the same physical level as your child.
4. Reflect and repeat back what he's saying and what he may be feeling to make sure you understand.

For example, when your son complains about something his teacher did at school, instead of saying, "Oh, c'mon. I'm sure it's not so bad. Mrs. Pierce is a great teacher" (which dismisses his thoughts and feelings), try something like, "That's tough! I'd be frustrated too." The second option reflects an understanding of his emotions—and helps him attach the word *frustration* to the jumble of feelings he's currently experiencing.

Emotional reflection

The fourth part of active listening is called "emotional reflection," which involves determining a person's feelings via their verbal and body language, labeling those emotions, and sharing those observations with the other person. It's a technique commonly used by therapists and counselors, as it increases trust and understanding.

The next time your son comes to you ranting after a video game loss, you can say, "You seem pretty angry—your face is red, and your voice is getting louder." If he responds by saying something like "No kidding! Of course I'm angry," reflect his words back to him again, matching the intensity of his voice: "Yes! You are very angry!"

It might feel counterproductive to simply label his emotions; you'll probably feel the need to *do something* instead. You might be tempted to take away his video game (or toss it out the window). But neither of those responses will help your son learn how to deal with the uncomfortable emotions that accompany losing.

By contrast, reflecting your son's emotions back to him helps him recognize his feelings—and that's the first step in learning how to deal with them.

Asking open-ended questions

A close-ended question is one that can be answered with a simple, often one-word response, such as *yes* or *no*. An open-ended question doesn't have a defined or easy response, and answering requires a bit of thought and creativity.

Whether you realize it or not, you already know that close-ended questions don't inspire conversation. Asking your son, "How was school today?" is rarely productive. Similarly, asking, "Was your math test as hard as you thought it was going to be?" isn't going to net you much detail. Try an open-ended question, such as, "What was the hardest part of your math test?"

Open-ended questions often start with one of the five "W" question words: *who, what, when, where, why*:

+ *Why do you think your brother hit you when you grabbed the iPad?*

+ *Where would you like to go if you could travel anywhere in the world?*

+ *What do you think will happen if you don't invite Max to your birthday party?*

Don't be surprised if your son answers, "I don't know." Tweens commonly use that phrase to mean, "I don't want to talk right now" or "I don't want to talk about this with you" or, sometimes, genuinely, "I don't know." Take a moment to assess the situation before responding. If your son is tired, hungry, or preoccupied, it's not a good idea to press him further. Instead, let the topic drop and revisit it later.

Jade's 11-year-old son discovered his Christmas gifts. All of them.

Thanks to his online snooping, there would be no surprises under the tree. Jade was seriously annoyed and disappointed. "I felt like he robbed me of the joy of watching him get a surprise on Christmas morning," she says. But instead of yelling at him or seething in silence, Jade, a veteran parent, decided to talk to her son about his discovery.

"I took a deep breath and asked him how he felt about it and why he did it," she says. His answer surprised her. "He said he didn't like surprises," Jade says. "He finds them stressful."

He hadn't mentioned his discomfort previously because he didn't want to disappoint his parents or ruin the family tradition. He hid his feelings to protect others.

Jade's calm, nonjudgmental, inquisitive questioning created a safe space for her son to express his true feelings. Understanding the emotion behind her son's behavior allowed Jade to respond productively.

"I told him that snooping for presents can take away joy from the present giver, and he really listened," she says. Together, they agreed to refocus their holiday celebration on family and food. Gifts remained a part of the holiday, but without expectation of surprise or joy. Her son felt relief, and so did Jade.

"Because I managed my emotions, I learned more about my son—and he learned that he can safely share his feelings with me," Jade says. "Accepting his feelings and not making a big deal out of the incident brought us closer."

Building Emotional Literacy Skills

Emotional literacy is the ability to identify, name, and communicate emotions. People who are emotionally literate can also recognize and respond to others' emotions.

Just as it takes time and making mistakes to learn how to read and write, it takes time and making mistakes to develop emotional literacy. Keep your expectations modest; 10-year-old boys are not the most emotionally astute human beings.

You can support your son's development by helping him understand the importance of emotional literacy. According to the late psychologist Claude Steiner, "Emotional literacy helps your emotions work for you, instead of against you." That's a concept your son can understand.

Here are two examples of sons who may not be aware of their own emotions.

Cool-down time improves emotional processing

Jack's face was red as he approached the car, but Trina, his mom, wasn't surprised. She knew Jack just had gym class and assumed his red face was the result of exertion.

But this time, Jack exploded when she said, "*Hello, how was school?*"

"Why do you ask me that all the time?" Jack said angrily.

Trina was stunned. Jack wasn't usually talkative after school, but he wasn't rude, either. She decided to try a different approach.

"What's wrong?" she asked, with a tone of concern.

"I don't know!" Jack said. His anger was palpable.

Trina didn't press. They drove in silence, and when they arrived home, Trina stayed quiet as Jack stomped up to his room. Twenty minutes later, she knocked on his door. "Snack delivery!" She placed a box of cheese crackers on the floor outside his room and walked away.

Approximately 45 minutes later, Jack came downstairs. "I'm sorry I was grumpy," he said.

"You were pretty upset," Trina responded.

"Yeah," Jack said. "Noah is moving."

"No way!" Trina said. "That stinks!" She knew Jack and Noah were close friends.

"Yep." Jack's eyes started to well up with tears.

"Are you sad about that?" Trina asked.

Jack nodded.

"I'll bet," Trina says. "I'd be sad too if my friend moved away."

"Yeah. I'm really going to miss him," Jack said. As he looked at his mom, a tear fell from his eye.

"It's okay to feel sad," Trina said, wrapping an arm around her son. "And it's okay to cry."

Reflection reveals the root of the problem

Sam slammed his bike to the ground. "I hate this stupid thing!" he said.

Claire looked up. She knew that Sam loved his bike; he spent every possible waking moment riding it. He'd recently developed an interest in bike tricks after he saw a few older boys land some impressive jumps at the park.

"What's wrong with your bike?" Claire asked.

"It's stupid!" Sam said, his voice rising.

"You sound pretty frustrated," Claire said. "What happened?"

"This bike is no good! These tires are garbage!"

"Oh?" Claire said.

"Yeah!" Sam said. "They're no good for wheelies!"

"No good for wheelies? What do you mean?"

"I can't stay up!" Sam said. "Not like those guys at the park! If I had better tires, I know I could."

"Oh, I see," Claire said, beginning to understand the situation. "You want to do wheelies and tricks as well as those other boys."

"Yeah!"

"You know, it's totally normal to feel frustrated and uncoordinated when you're learning something new," Claire said.

"I guess," Sam said.

"And sometimes, I feel a little scared when I try something new," Claire added. "Sometimes, I'm scared I won't be as good as I want to be."

"Yeah?"

"Yep," Claire said. "I don't like that feeling."

"Me, neither," Sam said. "The older boys made it look so easy."

"They did," Claire agreed. "But I'll bet it took them a long time to get that good."

"You think?"

"I do."

Practicing Problem Solving

Emotions are like alarms. Often, a strong emotional response is a sign that your unconscious has recognized a problem. That anger you feel when you come home after work and see dishes, clothes, and toys strewn all over the kitchen? That's an emotion pointing out a problem with work/life balance and chore assignments.

If you allow your emotion to distract you, you won't solve the problem. Instead, you'll start yelling at your family. Those brave enough to venture into the kitchen will do just enough to avoid further attack. You'll likely find yourself cleaning up most of the mess anyway.

But if you pause before responding—if you recognize your anger as an alarm—you can productively tackle the underlying problem. You (and any partner) can brainstorm and reassign household responsibilities, with your family's input. You can give yourself permission to create a new after-work routine.

When teaching your son, try this four-step approach to problem solving:

1. What am I feeling?
2. What's the problem?
3. What are the solutions?
4. What would happen if … ?

Here are two examples of a mom and a son practicing problem-solving skills.

Pinpointing homework problems

When Mateo threw down his pencil in the middle of homework, Susana braced herself. Homework was *always* a struggle.

Instead of immediately jumping in, though, Susana waited a beat.

"Ugh! I can't do this!" Mateo said.

"Sounds like you're frustrated," Susana said.

"This is too hard! Mr. Johnson never showed us how to do this part!"

"Oh, I see," said Susana. "You didn't go over this in class?"

"No!" Mateo exclaimed. "Well, kind of. But I can't remember any of it!"

Mateo's problem was becoming clear to his mother, but she wanted him to identify the problem as well.

"Do you think you forgot the instructions? Or did you not understand the material in class?"

"I don't know! Both!" Mateo said.

"I see," said his mother. "How do you think you can solve that problem?"

"I don't know," Mateo grumbled. "I'm stupid."

Susana knew Mateo's frustration was impeding his problem-solving abilities, so she offered a few suggestions. "What about texting a friend? Or asking Mr. Johnson first thing in the morning?"

"I guess I could ask Jack," Mateo said.

"Sounds like a plan," Susana said. "Let me know if you need anything else."

Solving a social dilemma

"No one ever picks me for their team!" Kai complained.

His mom's heart sunk. Their family had recently moved to a new community and Kai, a sports lover, was struggling with loneliness. Kate knew, from previous conversations with her son, that the boys often played soccer at recess—and that Kai hadn't been invited to play.

"Ugh!" Kate responded. "That stinks."

"Yep."

"What do you do when the other boys are playing?"

"I stand there and watch. I keep hoping they'll notice me and ask me to play, too."

"That would be nice," Kate agreed. "How's that worked so far?"

"Not very good," Kai said.

"What else could you try?"

"I don't know. I could ask? Or—I know!—I could just join in! I could go after that ball when it's near me!"

"What do you think the other boys would think of that?"

"Hmm. They might think I'm a ball hog," Kai said. "Or get mad at me for interrupting the game."

"Yeah. That's a possibility. What do you think would happen if you ask one of the guys if you can play?"

"I don't know. You know I hate talking to other people!"

Kai didn't like initiating conversation. So, Kate helped him brainstorm. Kai ultimately decided he'd bring his own soccer ball to school and start kicking it around at recess. He hoped the other guys would see his skill and invite him to play.

Kate wasn't sure Kai's plan would work, but she was proud of his problem-solving effort. If needed, they could always revisit the issue another time.

Coping with Negative Emotions

No one enjoys negative emotions. Sadness, anger, frustration, and shame simply don't *feel* good. We humans would much rather feel joy or contentment.

Yet negative emotions play an important role in our lives. The unpleasant feelings they generate are designed to motivate us. Negative emotions are a sign that something needs to change.

Unfortunately, many people learn to ignore negative emotions. As children, we learn that other kids don't like being around us when we're angry. Some of us learn that our family members don't like to see anyone crying. So, we hide our feelings.

But this allows problems to linger. In fact, ignoring bad feelings almost always makes things worse in the long run.

Teaching your son how to cope with negative emotions is one of the most important things you can do for him. Those who can recognize, accept, and process their emotions are generally happier and more resilient.

Anger

Michael Gurian, author of *The Wonder of Boys* and *Saving Our Sons,* says, "Anger is the most comfortable emotion for many boys today." Young boys are as likely as girls to feel and express sadness, fear, embarrassment, and joy. But years of hearing, "Big boys don't cry" and "Man up!" teaches them to suppress sadness and discomfort. Tween boys still feel pain, but before middle school, most boys have learned to transform hurt into anger.

Your primary job will to be to help your son identify the emotions hiding beneath his anger. Use active listening and emotional reflection techniques.

Sadness

Years of experience taught Thomas Hobson (aka "Teacher Tom") that sitting with a sad child is almost always helpful. As he wrote in a 2019 blog post, "The goal is not to end [the] crying, but to create a space in which he could finish his cry."

Many events—the loss of a friendship, not making a team, the death of a pet or family member—trigger sadness and your son, like all tween boys, is under intense social pressure to appear unbothered. Whenever possible, help him find a safe space to experience and express his sadness, even if that means hustling him out to the car quickly after team tryouts.

Frustration

Frustration is the feeling that arises when *something* is keeping us from achieving a goal. It's a common emotion for preteen boys because, for each one, their imagination tends to mature more quickly than their brain and body. They dream of doing great things, but their dreams often exceed their current skill level.

Help your son identify the obstacles and encourage him to brainstorm potential workarounds. Sometimes, stepping away from the problem when he feels frustrated is most productive; trying to push through a frustrating issue despite increasing irritation rarely works. Your son may discover a potential solution while riding his bike or shooting hoops. (Physical activity, by the way, helps calm frustration.)

Aggression

Aggression—hostile, violent behavior—is usually the result of extreme negative emotions. Unchecked anger can quickly spiral into aggression. So can shame and embarrassment.

Identifying and responding to negative emotions can keep boys from turning to aggression. So, if you teach your son to recognize the feelings associated with anger (for example, irritation, increased heart rate, a desire to run or hit) and what to do when he notices those feelings (take a few deep breaths, step away from the situation, punch a pillow, or run around the block), you may be able to help him avoid aggression.

Also helpful: plenty of time in nature. According to a 2019 *New York Times* article, research has shown that access to green space can decrease aggression.

Embarrassment

Preteen boys are easily embarrassed. Developmentally, they're inclined to believe that all eyes are on them, and they are super sensitive to others' opinions.

Unfortunately, boys' propensity for embarrassment peaks just as they're moving through their most awkward stage of life. They want to appear capable and confident at all times, but their body and brain betray them.

Role-model using humor to defuse embarrassment. If you accidentally splash your pants with water while doing dishes, for instance, instead of reacting with irritation, you can turn to your son, point to your pants, and say, "Oops! Looks like I wet my pants." Your son will learn that it's healthier to laugh at mistakes and mishaps—and that it's usually better to laugh at yourself than to wait for others to start pointing and laughing.

Paranoia

Paranoia is the unwarranted belief that others are out to get you.

It's normal for preteen boys to say things like "They all hate me!" or "My teacher doesn't like me; that's why I'm always in trouble and getting such bad grades." Most of the time, comments like these are just an attempt to shift blame and responsibility.

If your son is exhibiting true paranoia—if he insists on locking up his belongings because he's sure someone is trying to steal them or is convinced that his classmates are plotting against him—talk to his doctor or a mental health professional. Paranoia can be a symptom of mental illness (see "Identifying Mental Health Issues" on page 52).

Encouraging Creative Expression

Instinctively, most of us use the arts to manage our emotions. We cue our favorite songs when we want to boost our mood and turn on our favorite movies when we need a dose of comfort.

Art helps us channel and process our emotions. Making art is great for brain development, too. Engagement in the arts also increases self-confidence and decreases stress, anxiety, and depression.

Boys, though, face significant barriers to arts involvement. In many places, dance is considered "girly" or "gay," so boys steer clear to protect their status. Middle- and high school choirs, bands, art classes, and theater programs already skew female, which keeps more boys away, as they want to fit in with their male peers.

Your son will need your support and encouragement to remain engaged in the arts. Watch your language and encourage the men in your son's life to do the same; derogatory language about male artists can cripple a young boy's dreams. If your son demonstrates an interest in a specific art form, look for local or online classes, and see if his father or another male role model can help develop your son's creativity.

Musical instruments and singing

Got a son who constantly sings at home but refuses to join the school choir or the choir at your house of worship? Look for other outlets. Social singing apps (such as Smule) allow users to sing with others from the safety of home; karaoke apps are another option. Private vocal lessons, either online or in person, may be another alternative (try calling your local high school and asking if an older student might be interested in tutoring your son).

School bands and orchestras are a convenient, cost-effective way for tweens to learn to play a musical instrument. Boys who show interest in an instrument not offered at school can benefit from personal instruction. Your local music store may offer classes.

Drama and musical theater

Acting in a show—or helping backstage—can increase confidence, commitment, and communication skills. If your son's school doesn't offer a theater class or club, search for dramatic outlets or children's theaters. Some 4-H clubs offer dramatic opportunities, ranging from pantomime to improvisation and public speaking contests. You can also find drama classes online. (See "Resources," page 150, for more.)

Drawing, painting, and sculpting

You can encourage your son's involvement in the visual arts by providing arts materials—and tolerating mess! Keep paints, paper, colored pencils, markers, and sculpting clay on hand. Pull them out periodically; your son may join in if he sees you painting or sculpting at the kitchen table. Local studios and arts associations often offer low-cost art classes.

Remember: Art doesn't have to be perfect. Don't let a perceived lack of talent prevent you or your son from enjoying the process of creation.

Dancing

According to studies, 93 percent of boys involved in ballet reported teasing and name-calling; 68 percent experienced verbal or physical harassment and 11 percent were the victims of physical harm.

Boys who are interested in dance require intensive parental support and protection. Often, older men discourage boys' interest in dance, in part because they're well aware of the potential dangers. You can help your son by affirming his interest as valuable and important, and exposing him (and the other men in his life) to successful male dancers.

If your son is interested in dance class, look for boys-only classes. A boy who is the only male in a class full of girls may be more likely to quit than a boy who is surrounded by dancers who look like him.

Writing stories and poetry

Writing is a great way to process emotions. Unfortunately, the way writing is taught in school discourages many boys from doing it. Strict rules about grammar and punctuation stifle creativity, and many students are explicitly told that their stories can't include battles, weapons, or gore.

At home, allow your son to read and write whatever he wants (within reason; if your son is scared of ghosts, it's a good idea to steer him away from books about hauntings). Surround him with stories; audiobooks and podcasts are great options. Give your son a journal—and privacy. If he shares his stories or poetry with you, refrain from pointing out mistakes. Instead, applaud his effort and ask questions about the plot or characters.

TIPS FOR BUILDING SELF-CONFIDENCE

Praise what he gets right. It's so easy to focus and comment on all the things our boys do wrong. But you'll build his self-confidence and decrease conflict if you instead notice and praise the good things.

Ask him to do an important task just beyond his skill level. Boys love to make a meaningful difference in the world. Challenge your son by asking him to do something that might be a bit more than he can handle. If he likes to use tools, for instance, ask him to fix a loose doorknob.

Give him independence. Your son's not ready to go it alone, of course, but whenever possible, let him do things independently. By 12, he should be able to get himself up for school and make simple meals.

Identifying Mental Health Issues

As reported by journalist Katherine Reynolds Lewis in her book *The Good News about Bad Behavior*, one in two children will develop a mood or behavioral disorder, or substance addiction, by the time they turn 18. In 2019, nearly 10 percent of youth in the United States reported severe depression. Another study found the rate of adolescents experiencing depressive symptoms (such as feelings of worthlessness or guilt, decrease in pleasure, and sleep disturbances) increased by 52 percent in the 11 years prior to 2017.

The COVID-19 pandemic, which caused school shutdowns and community lockdowns, disrupting kids' connections to peers, extended family members, teachers, and coaches, didn't help. Mental Health

America noted a 9 percent increase in the average number of young people ages 11 to 17 accessing online mental health screenings in 2020.

Despite increasing awareness of the importance of mental health, many children and families still suffer in silence, in part because of lingering stigma. Some people still consider mental illness shameful, and traditional beliefs that equate mental illness with "weakness" make it especially difficult for men and boys to seek help. Another complication: Many people don't realize that boys can have eating disorders, too, or that frequent irritability is a common symptom of depression in boys.

A doctor or mental health professional can diagnose and treat mental health issues. Often, a visit to your primary care provider is a great first step, as your provider can check for possible physical explanations for concerning symptoms and conduct a basic mental health screening. You provider will also ask if there is a family history of depression, suicide, substance use, abuse, trauma, or mental illness. If so, you and your son may be at increased risk. Health-care providers and mental health professionals use standardized assessments to diagnose mental health disorders.

Diagnosis can point the way to treatment that can improve your son's quality of life.

Indicators of mental health issues

How do you know if your son has a problem with his mental health? Watch for these indicators:

+ Difficulty at school and changes in academic performance

+ Bullying other kids

+ Avoiding friends and family

+ Changes in energy levels

+ Frequent mood swings and outbursts

+ Lack of motivation

+ Decreased concentration or focus

+ Difficulty sleeping or sleeping much more than usual

+ Changes or loss in appetite; frequent stomachaches or headaches

+ Obsessing over appearance, weight, or body image

All kids, of course, experience an occasional lack of motivation. (So do adults!) And "frequent mood swing and outbursts" are a hallmark of puberty—as are changes in appetite and an increased focus on appearance.

What you're looking for is an overall pattern or out-of-character changes. Is your son behaving differently? Has his unusual behavior lasted for more than a few days? Talk to the other adults in his life to see what they've noticed.

Above all, pay attention to your gut feelings. If you think something is wrong, it probably is. It's best to seek professional advice.

Anxiety

According to the Brain & Behavior Research Foundation, between 15 percent and 30 percent of kids will experience an anxiety disorder before they turn 18. Statistically, girls are more likely to be diagnosed with anxiety, but many experts believe that disparity is because anxiety in boys may manifest as difficulty sleeping or angry outbursts. Boys may also attempt to hide their anxiety and "power through" because of social pressure to appear strong and in control.

The most common signs and symptoms of anxiety include:

+ Feelings of nervousness or irritability

+ Feelings of panic

+ A sense of impending danger or doom

+ Difficulty concentrating or sleeping

+ Increased heart rate or breathing, sweating, or shaking

+ Feelings of weakness or exhaustion

+ Frequent physical complaints, such as headaches or upset stomach

+ Avoidance of school or other activities

All humans feel anxious sometimes; a bit of anxiety can even be productive because it increases alertness. Anxiety turns into a problem when it interferes with daily functioning. If your son's anxiety keeps him from doing things he'd like to do, he may have an anxiety disorder.

Common anxiety disorders include generalized anxiety disorder (which affects 3 to 4 percent of children), panic disorder (which is characterized by panic attacks), social anxiety disorder, and separation anxiety disorder. Selective mutism, or an inability to speak in certain settings, is another type of anxiety disorder.

Treatment can ease anxiety and allow your son to fully experience life. If needed, doctors can also prescribe anti-anxiety medication.

Social phobias

Social phobias are another form of anxiety disorder. They are characterized by intense anxiety or fear of being judged or rejected in a social or performance situation.

Nearly all tweens are leery of being judged by their peers, and middle school–aged children frequently exhibit self-consciousness, insecurity, and a fear of appearing foolish in front of others. However, most kids can navigate everyday social situations without too much difficulty.

A child with a social phobia, though, may dread going to school. If the teacher calls on him in class, his heart rate may shoot up and he may feel dizzy, even if he knows the answer. He may decline invitations to birthday parties because going to someone else's house and meeting new people is too overwhelming.

Despite the disruption to their lives, most people who have a social phobia do not receive treatment. According to the Anxiety and Depression Association of America, more than one-third of people with social anxiety disorder experience symptoms for at least 10 years before seeking help.

Prompt diagnosis and treatment of social phobias can preserve an individual's self-confidence and social relationships. If your son experiences severe social anxiety, seek help ASAP. Without treatment, your son may miss out on crucial developmental experiences.

Depression

According to the Centers for Disease Control and Prevention (CDC), approximately 2 percent of kids between ages three and seventeen have been diagnosed with depression. Other studies have noted that depression is more common in teenagers than young children.

Common symptoms of depression include:

+ Changes in sleeping or eating patterns

+ Loss of interest in activities a person previously enjoyed

+ Feeling sad, hopeless, worthless, or guilty

+ Irritability

+ Decreased energy or restlessness

+ Difficulty concentrating

+ Self-harming behavior, such as cutting or other deliberate injury

+ Suicidal thoughts

Untreated depression can hinder a child's social and emotional development. Depressed children are less likely to form close friendships and learn new skills. They develop low self-esteem and a lack of motivation. In severe cases, untreated depression can lead to suicide. Though still rare, in 2018, suicide was the second leading cause of death among 10- to 34-year-olds.

If you have noticed symptoms of depression in your son, talk to him. Ask him what's going on. Depressive behavior after a loss (the death of grandparent or a pet, a friend moving away) is common.

The First-Time Mom's Guide to Raising Boys

However, depressive symptoms that last longer than two weeks may indicate a problem. Contact your child's health-care provider and let them know what you've been seeing at home. Ask for a depression screening.

If your son reports suicidal thoughts, say, "Thank you for trusting me and sharing that with me. We're going to get through this together." Then reach out for professional help. If he already has a therapist, contact the therapist; otherwise, call your physician. You can also call the National Suicide Prevention Lifeline at 800-273-TALK (8255) or text HOME to the Crisis Text Line at 741741.

Note: If your home contains firearms or weapons, they should be secured at all times.

Body image issues and eating disorders

As a woman, you know that physical appearance is constantly under scrutiny. What you may not realize is that boys also face unrealistic physical expectations. Surrounded by images of jacked-up guys with six-pack abs, many boys now exhibit symptoms of body dysmorphia, a body image disorder characterized by an obsession with perceived physical flaws. Some boys even develop eating disorders to try to reshape their bodies.

According to the Child Mind Institute, men account for approximately one-quarter to one-third of those struggling with eating disorders. In England, the number of annual hospital admissions for men with eating disorders has more than quadrupled since 2007.

Symptoms of eating disorders or body dysmorphia may include:

+ Excessive focus on exercising

+ Eating large amounts of food

+ Refusing certain food groups

+ Interest in nutritional supplements

+ Constant weigh-ins and frequent mirror checks

+ Extreme or rapid weight loss or gain

+ Rigid meal habits

+ Going to the bathroom right after meals

+ Unusual behavior during meals (such as cutting food into tiny pieces or pushing food around the plate)

It is normal for tween boys to eat a lot, and regular exercise is healthy. However, if your son's healthy habits are starting to seem more like an obsession, he may have body dysmorphia or an eating disorder. It's a good idea to share your concerns with your son's health-care provider, who can conduct a physical examination and mental health screening.

Effective treatment is available. However, many programs are geared primarily toward girls and young women. Look for a mental health professional who has experience working with boys.

Support for mental health

If you're feeling overwhelmed by all this information, take a deep breath. These problems have always been part of parenthood. The difference is that, in years past, mental health and emotional literacy weren't discussed. Today, we know that emotional well-being is the foundation of a healthy life, so teachers, parents, and others are consciously working to build kids' emotional intelligence. Thankfully, a plethora of resources are now available to parents everywhere.

Check to see if your son's school has a school counselor; if so, it's a good idea to introduce yourself, either via an email or in person at a parent/teacher conference or back-to-school night. School counselors can help parents and kids tackle behavioral issues, peer pressure, and academic challenges, and can refer families to other mental health professionals.

Most county health departments also have a Mental Health Services division. Counseling and substance use services may be available for a low fee.

Online classes and services are another alternative. Options include:

Youth mental health screening: Mental Health America's screening tools are reliable.

Online counseling: TalkSpace and Better Help are two online counseling services that will match you or your child with a counselor. Sessions can take place via video chat, phone, or text.

K'Bro: A free app/game that helps kids develop emotional resilience.

See **Resources** on page 150 for links and more. Important numbers to know:

National Suicide Prevention Lifeline: 800-273-TALK (8255) (available 24/7)

Substance Abuse and Mental Health Services Administration (SAMHSA) National Helpline: 1-800-662-HELP (4357) (available 24/7)

National Alliance on Mental Illness HelpLine: 1-800-950-NAMI (6264) (available Monday to Friday, 10 a.m.–8 p.m. ET)

National Eating Disorders Association Helpline: 800-931-2237 (available Monday to Thursday, 11 a.m.–9 p.m. ET, and Friday 11 a.m.–5 p.m. ET; if in crisis, text NEDA to 741741 to be connected to a trained volunteer)

FOR YOUR REFLECTION

1. What will you do to build your son's emotional literacy?
2. How will you help your son find safe outlets to express his emotions?
3. Is your son currently showing any signs of a mental health disorder? If so, what's your next step?
4. What mental health services are available in your community?

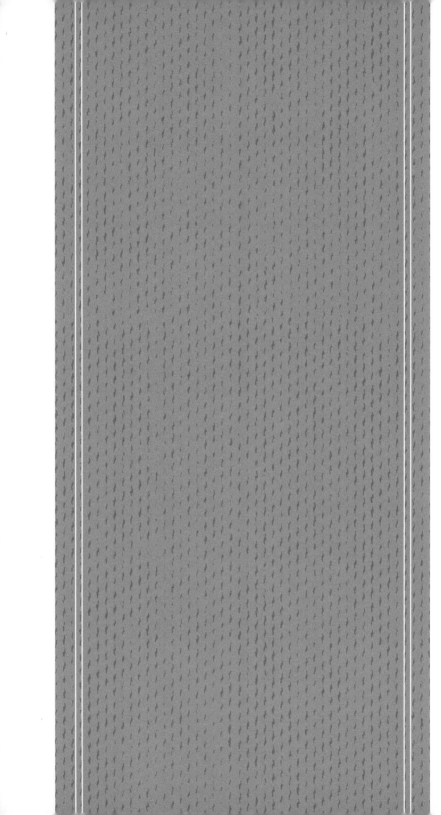

CHAPTER FOUR

Encouraging a Balanced Social Life

You are no longer the center of your son's life.

As you've probably already noticed, the boy who once proudly declared he'd marry you is now much more interested in spending time with his friends than with you. That's normal. And healthy.

Your son's friends will become increasingly important to him over the next few years. Their influence on him will be strong, but yours is as well. Although your son won't always acknowledge it, he's paying attention to everything you say and do. Now is a great time to talk about healthy and unhealthy relationships—and an excellent time to lay down some ground rules regarding online interactions and social media.

It's not easy to help your son develop a balanced social life. He'll resist your rules and make unwise choices. That's part of being a preteen. Your role is to love and support him.

Shifting Friend Groups and Roles

Boys develop social skills through their interactions with their peers. They learn about communication, conflict, trust, and loyalty, and they learn much about themselves as well.

In early childhood, friendships are often based on proximity and shared interests; your son's first friends were likely people in his class or neighborhood who liked to play the same things he did. In the tween years, boys become conscious of the social ramifications of friendship. They realize that some children are better-liked than others and they may try to gain favor with the "in" group to boost their social standing.

Social hierarchy and cliques

The dramatic physical and emotional changes kids go through around age 10 shake their self-confidence. Feeling unsure, they gravitate toward others. As *Washington Post* columnist Marguerite Kelly wrote, "The more uncertain they feel, the more they need to unite in self-defense."

This is not particularly problematic, as long as group members enjoy relatively equal standing. Problems arise when leaders establish spoken or unspoken rules that allow them to dictate group behavior. In a clique, leaders have the power to decide who is "in" and who is "out." Members who fail to conform to group expectations are shunned.

Their need for acceptance means that preteens are especially vulnerable to peer pressure. A boy who is craving social standing may bully or exclude other children if that's what it takes to stay in the clique's good graces, even if doing so causes him great personal distress or humiliates a childhood friend.

As much as you don't want to see your son become a "mean boy," avoid jumping to conclusions. Approach your son from a place of curiosity, rather than blame.

When you see your son doing something he wouldn't normally do to gain favor with friends, speak up. If your formerly basketball-loving son hasn't played in weeks, say something like *"You haven't played any basketball in a long time! Seems like you're always at the skate park with your friends instead. What's up with that?"*

Your son's answer will help you direct your conversation and give you a chance to point out that true friends allow you to be yourself.

When good friends go bad

Talk to your son early and often about the characteristics of healthy friendship. Tell him that true friends will accept him as he is, while unhealthy friendships are characterized by fear and distrust; a so-called "friend" might only "like" you if you do what he wants.

Watch for signs of friendship stress. According to a *Psychology Today* blog post by psychotherapist Erin Leonard, "Late-night tears, shrinking self-confidence, disinterest in previously cherished activities, and statements like, 'I hate myself'" can be signs that your child is part of a toxic friendship. If you notice any of these symptoms, talk with your son. Tell him what you see and ask what's going on. You may also want to talk to his teacher or coaches; they may have additional insight that could be helpful.

Similarly, if your son is spending time with a group of kids who make questionable and irresponsible decisions (graffitiing the local park, for instance), speak up. Begin with curiosity: "What do you like about spending time with that group of guys? Do they ever do anything that makes you uncomfortable?" Bring up your values: "You know that our family is all about respecting people and property." Listen to his answers, but don't be afraid to act. If you are concerned about a friend's influence on your son, minimize the amount of time they spend together. If a friend group seems problematic, steer him toward other activities he enjoys.

Being excluded

Preteens often use exclusion as a tool of social control. Psychologist Nicki Crick and research scientist Jennifer Grotpeter coined the term *relational aggression* in 1995 to describe behavior that intentionally damages someone's relationships or social status. Exclusion is a form of relational aggression and almost all children are affected. According to a survey by the Ophelia Project, 48 percent of students in grades five through twelve were regularly involved in or witnessed relational aggression.

Your heart will break when you see your son moping around after discovering online pictures of his friends at a party they didn't mention to him. Don't swoop in and try to solve the problem, though, and don't try to convince your son that those friends don't matter. Those friends *do* matter to him.

Do not reach out to his friends or their parents without first talking to your son. As a preteen, he likely does not need or want your help navigating friendships; instead, empathize with your son. You may be able to get the conversation going by saying something like "You usually hang out with your friends on Friday. Tonight you're home alone. What's up?"

Listen carefully to his answers; reflect his words and feelings. Together, brainstorm solutions to help him cope with his pain and address his exclusion. Possible solutions may include inviting other friends over, spending more time on a hobby, or honing his social skills.

Note: Many boys with ADHD and autism spectrum disorder struggle to recognize social cues and respond appropriately. Ryan Wexelblatt, a licensed clinical social worker, teaches boys social skills via his Dudes Learn Social series on his YouTube channel, ADHD Dude.

Parasocial online relationships

When you were a kid, you probably idolized an actress, musician, or athlete. You may have obsessively followed news about their career and decorated your locker with images of them.

You didn't know it at the time, but you were involved in a parasocial relationship—a one-sided relationship in which one person expends emotional energy and the other person is completely unaware of the first person's existence. Parasocial relationships are common in adolescence and may help preteens and teens develop their identity.

In the 21st century, it's common for boys to develop parasocial relationships with popular YouTubers and gamers. Although spending hours watching someone else play a video game may seem crazy to you, boys appreciate the gamer's skill and enjoy the feeling of familiarity they get while watching livestreams. In some cases, boys develop friendships with other followers and fans.

These online interactions may be positive. They give kids a chance to connect with others who share their interests and may contribute to a sense of belonging. However, your son needs real-world interactions as well. Some parents help their sons bring their online relationships into the real world. After her then–9-year-old son became deeply involved in the Gtramp community—a coalition of tween and teenage trampoline enthusiasts—mom Judi Ketteler took him to some meetups (and wrote about their experience for the *New York Times*). Her son's physical and social skills grew as a result; so did his self-confidence.

However, online relationships can also have a negative influence. Preteens' need to belong means they are highly vulnerable to peer pressure; if your son regularly hears corrosive language or racist and sexist opinions online, he's likely to parrot similar language and beliefs. Consider using parental controls and an internet filter (like Circle) to manage your son's online experience. Take the time to watch what he watches, and pay attention to recommended videos. Algorithms have a tendency to serve up increasingly intense content, so it's important to know what rabbit holes are being presented to your son as well.

Nigahiga. Ninja. Whistlindiesel.

At one time or another, my boys fanatically followed each of these YouTubers. Nigahiga (real name: Ryan Higa) produced funny videos with broad appeal; his classic "How to Hide a Fart" video has more than 16 million views. Ninja (Richard Tyler Blevins) rose to popularity as a gamer; my sons watched him stream many rounds of Fortnite. Whistlindiesel (Cody Detwiler) is best known for driving a modified Ford pickup truck into the Gulf of Mexico in late 2020, much to the delight of my now-teenage sons.

Get to know the influencers your son follows on social media. Ask him to show you his five favorite channels. Watch with him, instead of complaining when you see him online. Watch on your own too. He'll love the fact that you're taking an interest in his interests, and you'll be in a much better position to judge the appropriateness of the material he's consuming.

I don't love everything my boys encounter online. When I hear inappropriate language, I call it out and tell them to switch channels. When Ninja made headlines for using a racial slur, we talked about it. And when news broke that Logan Paul, a once-popular YouTuber, had posted a controversial video, I realized that my boys—fans of Logan—had probably seen the disturbing image. Our subsequent conversations weren't fun, but they were necessary.

Take an interest in your sons' online life. Establish a regular routine of sharing. For instance, one night a week, you might have each family member share a favorite YouTube video. These glimpses of your son's online activities will give you a more complete picture of his life.

Maintaining Strong Family Connections

Your son might be pulling away, but he's not ready for independence. He needs your steady presence in his life, and, although he won't admit it, he needs and wants the structure and stability in family routines.

Sharing family meals

Regular family meals are associated with lower rates of depression, anxiety, substance abuse, and eating disorders; they're also correlated with improved resilience and healthy self-esteem, according to a 2020 article posted by the Harvard Graduate School of Education.

Your meals don't have to be fancy; takeout from a local restaurant counts, as do PB&J sandwiches. You don't even need to gather the whole family daily. Simply gather whoever is home when it's time to eat. Sit down together; discuss. You can stoke conversation by asking questions such as "If you could see any musician, living or dead, who would you see?" or "What would you do with $1 million?"

Keeping routines together

If you don't build in together time, it's easy to drift apart. Do your best to keep up traditions and activities you both enjoy. If you've camped together for years, don't stop now; adjust your schedule and sneak in a camping trip when you can.

Consider creating new routines, like Friday night pizza-and-a-movie. Mundane chores can become bonding opportunities, too, if you add in some fun—perhaps a doughnut outing after Saturday morning cleanup?

Feel free to ditch traditions that bring on discomfort. If your holiday routines cause stress and conflict, scale back. Keep only the activities that bring you joy.

Create special moments

Life is hard, so take time to celebrate the special moments. Mark significant achievements (making a team, getting a good grade) with a special meal or a silly song. Some families have a special plate or cup that the honoree gets to use on noteworthy occasions.

Occasionally, turn an ordinary day into a remarkable one. Tom, a dad in Wisconsin, sometimes takes a vacation day from work and surprises his daughter with a daddy/daughter day. (They usually go out for breakfast and then visit a local attraction, such as the zoo.) Why not surprise your son with a mother/son day?

Brandy and Joe used to spend hours playing Legos together.

"I'd hear all about his favorite TV show and his favorite YouTubers," Brandy says. "It was my time to hear all the silly things [on] his mind."

Then Joe turned 12. His parents divorced and school got more stressful. Joe was no longer interested in Legos; he turned his attention to video games instead. Brandy was less than thrilled.

"I openly disapproved of the violence in his games," she recalls. "And I missed hearing about what was going on in his world. "

Instead of attacking or criticizing her son's interest in games, though, Brandy decided to join him.

"I realized it was up to me to engage in a new way with him," she says. "I started with What Remains of Edith Finch, an adventure game that's more like a book than a traditional video game. Next, I played Limbo, which is a dark puzzle-type game. That's when Joe got interested. He'd check on my progress and help with the hard puzzles."

Joe and Brandy started keeping each other company as they played, and Joe bought his mom a Microsoft gift card for Christmas so that she could buy Abzu, an underwater adventure game he was sure she'd like. Next up: Forza Horizon, a racing game the two plan to play together.

"I'm so grateful for the little moments these games have given us," Brandy says. "I've learned things about Joe I probably wouldn't have if I hadn't engaged in something way outside my comfort zone."

Conflict Management

Your son will get into fights with friends, arguments with you, and disagreements with his teachers. You'll both have lots of opportunities to try different conflict management skills.

Blaming, shaming, interrupting, and insulting are not effective conflict management techniques. These strategies almost never result in conflict resolution. Instead, they create more division.

Calmly expressing emotions and sharing facts, on the other hand, can result in understanding.

Role-modeling is the most effective tool you have to teach your son healthy conflict management strategies.

How to de-escalate and stop a fight

Small disagreements can quickly escalate to physical fights and long-standing feuds. Give your son some tools to de-escalate fights so that he can avoid trouble while maintaining his social standing.

For instance, if tempers flare while he's playing soccer because another boy claims your son deliberately tripped him, responding defensively—I did not!—will likely only make things worse. Instead, teach your son to offer consideration. Saying something like "My bad" and offering to redo the play may de-escalate the conflict.

Other strategies your son can use to de-escalate conflict include avoiding blame and validating others' feelings ("I can see you're upset, man").

How to walk away

Culturally, boys face a lot of pressure to fight, rather than walk away. Your son needs you to tell him that walking away isn't cowardly or weak, but a sign of maturity and strength. Teach him to take a deep breath when a fight is looming and ask himself one question: Is it worth it? In most cases, the answer will be no; the negative consequences of fighting (injury, disciplinary action) outweigh the potential benefits.

Give your son some phrases he can use to walk away: "I don't have time for this," "It's not worth it," "I'm sorry, man."

Tween boys are particularly vulnerable to peer pressure. When surrounded by other boys, young males tend to underestimate risk and overestimate potential rewards—which means that a boy who is adamantly anti-cigarette may decide to vape with friends in the school bathroom.

Teach your son some strategies he can use to resist peer pressure:

+ Say, "No thanks." And keep saying no: "Nope." "No way." "I said no."
+ Suggest another activity. ("I'd rather play video games.")
+ Leave.

If your son has a cell phone, decide on a code he can text you if he's in an uncomfortable, awkward, or difficult situation he'd rather not deal with. (Some parents use "X.") When he sends you the code, call him immediately and tell him he must come home ASAP. Your son can blame you and leave the situation.

Bullying

Approximately one in five tweens experiences bullying.

Boys are more likely than girls to be the victims of physical bullying, which may include being pushed, shoved, hit, tripped, or spit on. Destruction of personal property is another form of physical bullying.

Boys can also experience emotional bullying, which includes being humiliated, ridiculed, or intentionally excluded. Sometimes, bullies force their victims to do something they do not want to do. Cyberbullying, which occurs online or via text, may involve rumors, lies, and physical threats. Boys are much more likely than girls to receive threats of violence online.

As a result of anti-bullying campaigns in recent years, most kids are well-acquainted with the term *bullying*—but many are confused about the difference between bullying and teasing. According to the CDC and the US Department of Education, bullying involves unwanted aggressive behavior and an imbalance of power. Two friends calling each other names isn't bullying; a popular student repeatedly taking over another student's seat on the bus may be bullying.

Signs that your son is being bullied

Your son probably won't tell you if he's being bullied. At least not in so many words.

Boys who are bullied may hide their experience because they don't want their parents to know they're "losers." Some are afraid of their parents' reaction. They don't want to see disappointment reflected in their parents' faces, and they definitely don't want Mom or Dad coming to school to confront the bully.

The first signs of bullying may be subtle—and easy to misinterpret. Frequent headaches and stomachaches, for instance, may be signs of bullying. So can refusal to go to school or declining grades. Other possible symptoms include:

+ Unexplained injuries or bruises

+ Lost or destroyed clothing or possessions

+ Changes in eating habits, such as skipping meals or binge eating

+ Difficulty sleeping or frequent nightmares

+ Sudden loss of friends or avoidance of social situations

+ Change in demeanor (a formerly happy-go-lucky kid may become increasingly anxious)

+ Unusual after-school behavior

According to Peggy Moss, a nationally known expert on bullying, the boys' bathroom is a frequent site of torment, as teachers typically steer clear of that space. As a result, boys who are being bullied may avoid using the restroom at school. If your son rushes straight to the bathroom every day after school, set aside time for a chat. Similarly, if your son seems much hungrier than usual after school, it's possible he's not eating lunch, either because a bully is taking his lunch or because your son is avoiding the cafeteria altogether in hopes of avoiding his bullies.

Note: Never make assumptions. Your tween might be hungry after school because he's going through a growth spurt. So, begin by simply stating your observations: "Wow, you're a lot hungrier than usual!"

What to do if your son is being bullied

Do not overreact. The last thing your son wants is you storming into school.

Also, don't underreact. Your son needs to know that you take his concerns seriously.

Remain calm and levelheaded; if you start getting visibly upset, your son will likely stop talking with you. Instead, practice your active listening skills. Reflect your son's words back to him; ask for clarification.

Avoid the impulse to offer solutions. Bullying has already made your son feel weak and insecure, and if you swoop in and solve the problem for him, he'll suffer additional ridicule and a loss of confidence. Encourage him to brainstorm solutions by asking something like this: "What could you say or do next time that happens?" When he suggests alternatives, help him work through possible outcomes by asking, "What do you think will happen if you do that?"

If you or his other parent stood up to a bully as a child, it may be useful to share your story with your son. He needs to know that people can thrive despite bullying.

Talk to his teacher if the bullying is taking place at school. Do so discreetly, however. Call, email, or text his teacher and ask for an appointment. When you meet, do not bring your son along. Stay calm and share what he's told you, as well as your observations. Don't be surprised if the teacher is unaware of the bullying; most bullying behavior takes place far from teachers. Ask the teacher to monitor the situation and act as needed.

If nothing changes in a week or so, contact the school principal or counselor. Let them know that you talked to the teacher and share your son's experience. Ask, "What's the next step?" Establish a follow-up date.

If the bullying persists despite conversations with your son's teacher and principal, call the district superintendent and ask for a meeting.

CONVERSATION STARTERS WITH YOUR SON

→ "I've heard a lot about bullying lately. What's going on at your school?"

→ "You don't seem like yourself. Has something changed?"

→ "What do you usually do at recess time? What do the other kids do?"

→ "Who is the meanest person in your class?"

What to do if your son is bullying
Breathe.

If you hear that your son is bullying others, take a moment before talking with your son. It's easy to blame yourself, but the truth is that kids bully for all kinds of reasons. Some kids bully others to gain acceptance, or because they'd rather bully than be bullied. Some are looking for attention. Others are repeating behaviors they've seen elsewhere.

Approach your son calmly. Tell him what you've heard and ask what's going on. Listen carefully to his answer; the situation may be more complex than you initially realized. However, do not excuse bullying behavior. Reiterate your family values and let him know that you will not tolerate physical or emotional aggression. (You'll probably have to put that in kid-friendly terms for him. Example: "It's not okay to tell people that Jake wet his pants.")

Try to help your son understand how his behavior affects other people. How would he feel, for instance, if no one wanted to spend time with him because someone spread a nasty rumor about him?

Establish a meaningful consequence. If your son is verbally harassing other kids while playing video games online, take away his game console for a time. Similarly, if your son has been threatening others via social media, restricting his internet access is reasonable. If his school is taking disciplinary action, support the school, rather than arguing your son's point.

Some kids who bully are repeating patterns they've seen at home or elsewhere. Think about who your son interacts with. Does he spend time with anyone who intimidates or mistreats others? If so, you may need the help of his school counselor or a private therapist to get to the root of the issue and help him develop healthier ways of interacting with his peers.

Monitor your son's behavior. Don't take him at his word if he tells you, "Things are better now." Instead, check with his teacher or the parents of the affected child. If the bullying behavior persists, seek professional help. Your son's school counselor may be able to suggest local resources.

Supporting an Introvert

Are you an introvert or an extrovert?

Introverts draw energy from being alone; extroverts draw energy from other people. Understanding your basic personality type—and your son's—can help you parent him effectively.

Introverts need time alone to recharge. They may hang to the side in social situations, preferring to observe before joining in. They may be uncomfortable meeting new people or going to unfamiliar places. Introverts are often deep thinkers who prefer to express themselves via art, music, or the written word, rather than verbally.

If you're an introvert, supporting an introvert son may be easy. After all, you both need quiet time and solitude, and you probably understand your son's hesitation when he's invited to a classmate's birthday party. If you're an extrovert, you probably worry about your son's tendency to spend time alone or with just a few close friends.

The world needs both introverts and extroverts. Accepting your son as he is will allow him to flourish. He'll learn how to work with his personality, instead of feeling that there's something wrong with him.

Plan ahead before social interactions

Social situations are stressful for introverts. They do better if they know what to expect. So, give your son as much detail as possible before social events. Let him know who will be there and describe what will likely happen during the event.

Role-playing can help some children. If your son is attending a party at a friend's house, help him brainstorm and practice a few phrases he can use when he meets new people. ("I'm José's friend. How do you know him?") Together, think of ways he can step away from the activity if he becomes overwhelmed. (Bathroom breaks can give introverts a chance to regroup.)

Don't push too hard

Pressuring your son to "get out more" will only increase his anxiety and drive a wedge between you. A child who says he'd rather stay home and read than go to a baseball game is not being rude or ungrateful; he's simply expressing his preference. Introverts need more time alone than most extroverts can possibly imagine.

Praising your son when he successfully navigates an uncomfortable social situation may increase his confidence. Try saying something like this: "I know it took a lot of courage for you to try out for the team. I'm really proud of you" or "Sounds like you had fun at the party, even though you were nervous about going."

Encourage participation in clubs and activities

Involvement in a club or other extracurricular activity centered on one of your son's passions or skills can help him connect with other people who share his interests.

A boy who loves to draw, for instance, might happily participate in a community mural event.

If your son has a close friend who shares similar interests, consider encouraging them to join a club together. Your son may feel more comfortable attending if he knows at least one person in the room.

Supporting an Extrovert

Extroverts need human interaction to function at their best. They tend to think out loud and don't like playing alone. Extroverts can be high energy and usually have a lot of friends.

Parenting an extrovert means helping your child meet his need for social interaction while also teaching him to tolerate time alone. Frequent playdates are good for your son; he'll be most content if he gets to spend some time with friends each day. Organized clubs and activities can give your son additional opportunities to connect with others.

Extroverts work most efficiently when they are surrounded by other people. So, don't send your extroverted son to his room to do homework; instead, let him work at the kitchen table while you make dinner. He'll be energized by your presence. Similarly, asking your son to clean the garage alone won't be nearly as effective as working beside him.

If you're an introvert, parenting an extrovert can seem exhausting—your son wants nearly constant human interaction, and you want (and need) frequent alone time. Timers and concentrated attention can help. When you need time alone, tell your son that you want to spend some time with him first. Set a timer for 10 minutes or so and give him your complete attention. When the timer goes off, encourage your son to engage in an activity he enjoys and excuse yourself to another room. Set a timer again and tell your son he can't disturb you until after it beeps.

Learning to respect others' needs is an important step on the path to maturity.

FOR YOUR REFLECTION

1. Were you popular or unpopular in middle school? How do you think your experience will influence your parenting?
2. Do you think boys should "fight back"? Why or why not?
3. How will you help your son navigate uncomfortable social situations?

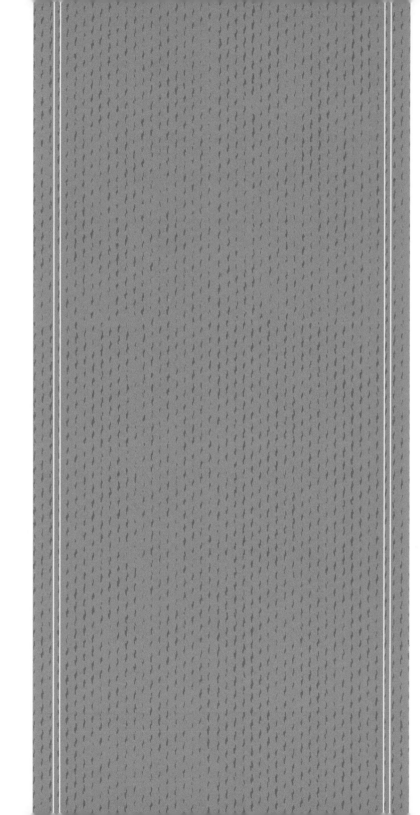

CHAPTER FIVE

Facilitating Learning

School is a *major* source of conflict between parents and their tween sons.

It doesn't have to be, though. Learning about boys' educational experiences and understanding the difference between real learning and forced academics will allow you to facilitate your son's intellectual growth without quashing his spirit.

First things first: School has changed a lot since you were a student. Five-year-old boys are now expected to read and write, even though their brains and bodies aren't necessarily developmentally mature enough to handle those tasks. Young boys who struggle with reading and writing, and are punished for their natural inclination toward movement, quickly conclude that school is "not for them." By third grade, many boys have mentally checked out of school.

You may have to dig deep to discover impediments to your son's learning. It's worth the effort, though. Addressing your son's academic challenges now will make his teen years easier for both of you.

The Role of Agency in Self-Directed Learning

Between ages 8 and 12, boys' vocabulary increases dramatically. They start to think abstractly and apply logic and reasoning to problems. As their ability to focus grows, so does their capacity to consider multiple perspectives.

Because of tweens' increasing ability to process and analyze information, students in seventh grade, for instance, are expected to cite pieces of textual evidence, scrutinize interactions, and reason abstractly and quantitatively.

The problem is that boys are rarely asked to apply these skills to topics that interest them. Boys crave real-world experiences; they want to make a difference. And solving for x? Well, most boys can (and will) effectively solve equations when the numbers matter to *them*—when trying to figure out how much money they'll make mowing lawns or how many quarts of oil are needed to maintain a dirt bike during riding season. But ask them to solve for x for no other reason than "school is important" and most boys will exert little to no effort.

The more opportunities you can give your son to develop his reading, writing, speaking, listening, and reasoning abilities via avenues that interest *him*, the more your son will learn. Giving your son space to explore his interests is one way you can help him become a self-directed learner who takes initiative to formulate goals and seek resources to achieve them.

Exploring and being curious

The best learning is fueled by genuine curiosity. Notice and encourage your son's sparks of interest. If he's fascinated by sharks, schedule a trip to a local aquarium or cue up a shark documentary. When he asks a question you can't answer, suggest that he look online. Let him search and share his findings with you.

It's easy to support your son's curiosity when his interests align with yours. It's more difficult when your son is engrossed by a topic that's of no interest to you. However, it's important to encourage his exploration despite your lack of interest. Loving your son may mean watching and listening attentively as he shows you his latest *Minecraft* creation or helping him plant and care for a garden, even if you hate getting dirty.

Asking questions

According to a 2018 study by researchers from the University of Michigan C.S. Mott Children's Hospital and the Center for Human Growth and Development, children who ask a lot of questions do far better in school than children who sit quietly and wait for information to be delivered to them.

Unfortunately, many schools still subscribe to the "sit down, shut up, and learn" model of education. All too often, well-meaning teachers, desperate to get through the curriculum, shut down students' questions. Eventually, students stop asking.

You can keep your son's curiosity alive by encouraging and entertaining his questions. Pay attention to sentences that start with "Why" or "I wonder"; those words are clues that your son is trying to figure something out. Join him in his exploration. ("I've always wondered that, too! I'm not sure why the water looks so blue some days and not others.")

Verbalizing your own curiosity and questions, rather than going straight to Google, may help your son realize that asking questions (and not having all the answers) is natural and normal.

Offering ideas

Children have tremendous insight and ideas, and can imagine possibilities we can't. And yet, many adults are quick to quash kids' ideas.

While it's true that you have more life experience than your son, he'll learn more if you allow him to offer and explore ideas. Need to figure out how to keep the squirrels from eating all the birdseed in your backyard bird feeder? Ask your son to help you brainstorm solutions. Don't call any of his ideas "crazy" or "not practical." Instead, ask questions to help him think through possibilities and problems. ("What do you think will happen if you do that?") Give him the necessary materials and support to construct his squirrel defense system, for instance, and watch learning unfold in real time.

Learning from mistakes

Your son will most certainly make mistakes. (So will you.) His first attempt at a squirrel defense system probably won't work. But he can learn from his mistakes—if you role-model acceptance of mistakes as a natural part of life and encourage him to try again.

Instead of reacting with anger or frustration when you or he messes up, try saying something like, "Whoops! Guess that didn't work!" and "What should we try next time?" Discuss the fact that most marvelous creations—from books and the iPad, to dirt bikes and video games—are the product of multiple iterations. Creators get an idea, make something, try it out, get feedback from others, and revise their creation based on what works and what doesn't. Teach your son that mistakes give him information he can use to move forward.

12 BOOKS TO READ BEFORE 12

Because reading proficiency varies greatly among children of the same age, schools often use Lexile levels to describe a child's ability to read and understand text. Your son may already know his Lexile level; if so, look for books around his level. If a book is too difficult for your child to read independently, consider reading it together.

Bridge to Terabithia by Katherine Paterson
Jesse befriends a new girl, Leslie, and learns about life and loss. Ages 8–12; Lexile level 810.

The Chronicles of Narnia by C. S. Lewis
In this seven-book series, a wardrobe is a magical portal to a world of adventure. Ages 8 and up; Lexile level 870.

Ender's Game by Orsen Scott Card
A boy genius trains to crush an alien invasion. Ages 10–12; Lexile level 780.

Hatchet by Gary Paulsen
Thirteen-year-old Brian must make it on his own in the wilderness after a plane crash. Ages 12–14; Lexile level 1020.

It's Trevor Noah: Born a Crime: Stories from a South African Childhood by Trevor Noah
An adaptation for young people of the *Daily Show* host's autobiography, describing his experiences growing up as a mixed-race child in apartheid-era South Africa. Ages 10–17; Lexile level 780.

The Lightning Thief by Rick Riordan
Boys love this book because it features an unlikely hero (with ADHD traits), as well as an action-packed story line. Ages 9–12; Lexile level 680.

Now or Never! 54th Massachusetts Infantry's War to End Slavery by Ray Anthony Shepard
Dual biography of two extraordinary African American Union soldiers. Ages 10–17; Lexile level 1140.

The One and Only Ivan by Katherine Applegate
Based on a true story, this book explores friendship, love, and healing through the eyes of Ivan, a gorilla. Ages 8–12; Lexile level 540.

12 Rounds to Glory: The Story of Muhammad Ali by Charles R. Smith Jr.
Rap-inspired verse tells the tale of the famous boxer turned activist. Ages 10–12; Lexile level NP (non-prose).

The Warrior Kid series by Jocko Willink
Written by a Navy SEAL, these fun books teach boys what true strength and discipline look like. Ages 8–12; Lexile level 610.

The Watsons Go to Birmingham—1963 by Christopher Paul Curtis
Fiction and history collide in this book, which tells the story of the (weird) Watson family and their trip to Birmingham, Alabama, at one of the darkest moments in American history. Ages 8–12; Lexile level 920.

Wonder by R. J. Palacio
Named one of *Time* magazine's 100 Best Young Adult Books of All Time, *Wonder* features a main character who looks different but just wants to fit in. Ages 6–14; Lexile level 790.

Appreciating Neurodiversity

No two brains are alike.

They pretty much all have the same components—a frontal lobe, a cerebellum, etc.—but the "wiring" within each of our brains is unique and influenced by our genetics and experience. The term *neurodiversity* refers to the range of differences in human brain function; it highlights the fact that variations in sociability, learning, attention, and mood are normal and expected.

The brains of people with autism spectrum disorder and ADHD function differently than the brains of people who do not have autism or ADHD. Their brains are not flawed, just different. Appreciating neuro-diversity can allow you to embrace differences in learning. There's nothing "wrong" with a person who has dyslexia, autism, ADHD, or dyscalculia (difficulty understanding and manipulating numbers); they simply need teachers and parents who respect their particular needs. All humans flourish with appropriate support.

Dyslexia

According to the Mayo Clinic, dyslexia is a learning disorder that makes reading difficult "due to problems identifying speech sounds and learning how they relate to letters and words." Symptoms may include difficulty reading; unusual difficulty in handwriting and spelling; rever-sals and transpositions of letters in writing; difficulty discriminating among similar speech sounds; and poor recall ability.

Dyslexia is a neurological issue; it is *not* caused by laziness or lack of motivation.

In the United States, schools have a legal obligation to help children diagnosed with dyslexia. Necessary supports may include phonics-based reading instruction, speech therapy, tutoring sessions with a reading specialist, extra time to complete tests and assignments, and alternative ways to demonstrate learning.

If you think your son may have dyslexia, consider having him tested. You can find free dyslexia screening tests online. To receive accommodations at school, your child will likely need a professional assessment and diagnosis. Look for a child psychologist, a neuro-psychologist, or an educational psychologist who specializes in dyslexia. Your son's doctor or school counselor may be able to point you to local resources.

Dyscalculia

Dyscalculia is a math learning disability characterized by difficulty processing and working with numbers. A person may have a hard time comparing two amounts or recognizing quantities without counting. They may have difficulty recalling basic math facts (like multiplication and division tables) and may struggle with estimating, counting change, and telling time.

Like dyslexia, dyscalculia is neurological. Dyscalculia and dyslexia often occur together. According to an article published in *ADDitude* magazine, approximately half of all children with dyscalculia also have dyslexia.

There is no cure for dyscalculia, but intervention can help affected individuals manage math. Without intervention, most people with dyscalculia will have continued difficulty throughout life, which may inhibit their ability to work and handle personal finances.

Multisensory math instruction—which often involves allowing children to physically manipulate objects to solve problems—can help. Some schools already use this form of instruction. At others, you may have to request multisensory math tutoring. You can also request class-room accommodations, including extra time to take tests and the right to use a calculator. At home, playing board games with your child is one way to build numeracy skills.

ADHD

Attention-deficit/hyperactivity disorder (ADHD) has been diagnosed in nearly 10 percent of American children, according to the CDC. Boys are two times more likely than girls to be diagnosed with ADHD, though some experts believe that's because girls are more likely to have the inattentive form (characterized by daydreaming) and boys are more likely to have the hyperactive version, characterized by classroom-disrupting behaviors that catch teachers' attention.

Boys with ADHD struggle to maintain focus and attention during non-preferred tasks. They can play video games or build with Legos for hours, if that's what interests them, but struggle to put away a backpack without getting distracted. The condition also makes it difficult for children to regulate their emotions and plan for the future.

Medication and behavioral therapy can help boys (and their families) cope with ADHD. Though some people believe boys are overmedicated for ADHD, the scientific evidence is clear: Medication improves symptoms in 70 to 80 percent of individuals, and those who are treated with medication are less likely to develop substance use problems and may perform better in school.

A psychiatrist or neurologist can prescribe and tweak ADHD medication. Psychologists and licensed therapists who specialize in treating ADHD can help boys develop their executive function skills.

Autism

According to the CDC, 1 in 54 eight-year-old children in the United States is diagnosed with an autism spectrum disorder (ASD). Boys are four times more likely than girls to be diagnosed with autism, although recent research suggests this may be because of poor diagnostic tools, rather than boys being at greater risk.

ASD is characterized by challenges with social skills, repetitive behaviors, and communication. Symptoms and severity vary. According to Autism Speaks, an autism advocacy organization:

+ Nearly half of those with autism wander or bolt from safe places

+ More than a quarter of affected children self-injure via activities such as head banging, arm biting, or skin scratching

+ More than half struggle with sleep

+ Nearly two-thirds have been bullied

Interventions and support must be tailored to the needs of the child and family. Children with ASD qualify for individualized education plans (IEPs) at school, which detail interventions staff will use to help your child learn. Interventions may include speech therapy, occupational therapy, instructional aides, frequent breaks to move around, and the right to leave the classroom as needed for a safe space to decompress.

How to Help Your Son in School

Generally, boys do worse in school than girls. According to the Organisation for Economic Co-operation and Development (OECD), there has been a "reversal of the gender gap in education" over the past few decades. In most industrialized countries, boys now lag behind girls academically. Female students typically earn higher grades than male students and graduate from high school and college at greater rates than males. Boys, meanwhile, account for the vast majority of school discipline referrals and are about twice as likely as girls to be suspended from school. The majority of students in special education classes are also boys.

By age 8, many boys are anti-school. In 1980, 14 percent of surveyed male students told researchers they "didn't like" school. By 2001, 24 percent said they didn't like school. That number is likely even higher today, as pandemic-inspired virtual learning has caused additional stress for boys and their families.

Understanding why boys struggle in school is step 1 toward helping your son survive middle school and high school. Step 2 is tuning in to *your* son: How does he feel about school? What's his experience like?

Understand his motivation

Preteen boys don't care nearly as much about academics as their parents do.

The sooner you acknowledge that fact, the sooner you can begin working with your son. For him, school is all about socialization. He wants to fit in; he does not want to go against established social norms and risk getting ostracized.

Unfortunately, boys face a lot of peer pressure to *not* do well in school. According to a 2020 article published in *Social Psychology of Education*, high school boys are 1.5 times as likely as girls to say they will be ridiculed for trying hard in school and nearly twice as likely to say they'd be unpopular if they did so. Many boys actively limit their academic effort to maintain social standing.

So, you'll have to help your son find his motivation for learning. One way you can do so: Link his interests to academic subjects and his classroom assignments to real-world projects. If your son is interested in baseball, but struggling in math, introduce him to baseball statistics. If he has to write a paper for his language arts class, encourage him to write about snowmobiles or dance or his favorite YouTube channel.

CONVERSATION STARTERS

→ "What do you want to get better at this year?"

→ "At your school, is there any overlap between the popular kids and the smart kids?"

→ "Why do you think there are more girls than boys on the honor roll?"

→ "If you could learn about anything you wanted at school, what would you learn?"

Create goals, rewards, and consequences

Most preteen boys are focused on the here and now. They care about friends and family. They want to fit in and do things they enjoy.

However, you can still work with your son to create academic goals that align with his motivation. Got an athlete? Likely, his school requires a minimum GPA for participation in school sports. If not—or if your son is capable of much more than the bare minimum—decide together, as a family, what academic expectations your son must meet to participate in sports. You may decide, for instance, that he must have all assignments turned in before attending practice or games.

Many parents of tweens link video game time to academics, as most boys are highly motivated to connect with friends via gaming. Some parents allow boys extra game time if they do exceptionally well on a test or in a class. Other parents restrict game time if their sons fail to meet academic expectations. Still others allow gaming only after their son finishes his homework and they have checked that it's done.

Work together to draw up a clear contract that reflects your son's goals and your expectations. Be sure to incorporate your son's ideas and do not hesitate to enforce agreed-upon consequences when necessary.

Stick to structure

Most preteen boys aren't great at time management or organization, so homework can be a struggle.

Instead of nagging your son about his schoolwork every single day, work with him to create a homework routine. Note: Doing homework right after school is *not* the best option for most boys. Most need time to de-stress from the school day first. Your son may want to head straight to his video games, but physical activity is a better after-school/before homework option than digital activities. Movement allows a boy to burn off stress hormones and gets his brain ready to learn. Consider encouraging at least a half hour of outdoor activity before homework time.

Allow your son to decide where he'd like to do his homework. Some boys do best at a desk in a quiet room; most do not. A few do well in complete silence; many prefer background music.

Shorter homework sessions may be more effective than longer ones. Try setting a timer for 15 or 20 minutes and allowing your son some "fun" breaks between homework sessions.

Addressing overachieving and perfectionism

Perfectionism can look a lot like procrastination. Children who want to get everything "just right" often avoid starting assignments; when they begin, they may work slowly and spend a lot of time redoing good work in hopes of making it better. They may even miss deadlines because they refuse to turn in a project that is less than perfect.

Overachievers and perfectionists mistakenly think that their worth is a function of their work—in other words, they believe that they're only worthy of love if they meet (or exceed) expectations. Unwittingly, many parents and teachers fuel perfectionism by constantly emphasizing achievement and excellence.

You certainly want your son to reach his potential, but all children need to know that "good enough" is sometimes okay. Ask your son, "Is putting in an extra two hours of work worth an extra five points?" When he shares a project or assignment with you, don't immediately point out his mistakes. Instead, compliment his effort.

In many cases, perfectionism is rooted in anxiety. If your son's quest for perfection is causing him distress, consult a therapist or a mental health professional.

> James was a "clever, inquisitive, vivacious, and optimistic learner" when he started kindergarten at age five-and-a-half, says his mother, Leah. But he was also a full-body learner, the kind of kid who learned best while moving. His kindergarten teacher, though, preferred students who remained still and obeyed her commands. James's love of learning took a hit and his self-esteem started to decline.
>
> His early elementary years weren't much better. A couple of teachers "got him," Leah says, and in their classes, James thrived. School, though, was becoming a struggle.
>
> At age 9, standardized testing revealed James's great intelligence: His test scores for both math and literacy were in the top 5 percent. However, over the next six years, his grades gradually dropped.
>
> "The huge potential and promise he showed in his early years was quashed, I believe, by teachers who didn't know how to embrace his way of learning or his individual needs," Leah says. In hindsight, she wishes she'd been a more forceful advocate for her son, who was eventually diagnosed with ADHD.
>
> "If your son is losing his love of learning, take action," she advises. Seek professional help; an earlier ADHD diagnosis may have pointed to interventions that would have helped James thrive.

Addressing Defiant Behavior at School

No parent likes getting phone calls or emails from school about their son's misbehavior. If you have a son, though, you'll almost certainly get one (or more) of these messages.

Forgetting an assignment, of course, is not a big deal. And neither is saying no to the teacher when asked to do something. Very often, tween boys will experiment with "smart talk" in an attempt to impress their peers. Most stop when teachers and parents let them know that such behavior is unacceptable. (In some cases, the lesson doesn't sink in until boys experience a negative consequence, such as loss of video game playing privileges for a period of time.)

Boys who are consistently defiant at school—who regularly rebel against their teachers' instructions, speak rudely to others, and explode when reprimanded—may have oppositional defiant disorder (ODD), a condition characterized by a pattern of disobedience and hostility toward authority figures. According to a *Medscape* article, 1 to 11 percent of people have ODD and preteen boys are more likely to have it than girls.

All children, of course—and tween boys, especially—experience occasional bouts of defiance, anger, and disobedience. If defiant and argumentative behavior has been an issue for six months or more, though, you may need professional assistance. Your child's primary health-care provider or school counselor may be able to refer you to a mental health professional who can holistically evaluate your son. Professional evaluation is important because many kids with ODD also have ADHD, depression, anxiety, or a learning disorder.

Family therapy, social skills training, cognitive problem-solving training, and parent-child interaction therapy can all reduce defiant behavior in children who have been diagnosed with ODD. Look for professionals who specialize in working with children with ODD, and be sure to share behavior management strategies with your son's teachers.

Most preteens lie to avoid negative consequences.

When you catch your son in a lie, don't argue with him. Instead, simply state what you saw or know to be true. ("Mrs. Smith told me you haven't handed in your science project.") If you can't state the facts calmly, step away and take a break before dealing with your son.

Give your son an opportunity to share his side of the story; then, decide on a consequence. (You can take a break between talking and issuing a consequence, too, if needed.) You may want to ask your son what he thinks an appropriate consequence would be; many times, boys come up with effective ideas. Apply the consequence and move on with your lives. Repeat as necessary.

Dealing with Distractions

Learning to deal with digital distractions is an essential 21st-century skill.

Schoolwork often occurs on computers a few clicks away from nearly every movie ever made, as well as most of the people you've ever met, and an infinite number of funny memes and cat videos.

Devoting significant time to helping your son manage distractions will help him flourish in the digital world. Right now, he needs you to establish some guardrails while he develops the capacity to self-regulate. You'll have the best success if you collaborate with him to create some agreed-upon guidelines.

Make it clear that you respect (and will honor) your son's desire to play video games and connect with friends virtually. Try saying something like this: "Hey, I know it's important for you to play games with your friends" or "I know you love watching car videos on YouTube and want to make sure you have time for that." Emphasize the importance of including physical activity, outdoor time, and family time in each and every day. Work together to create rules around the following topics.

Video games

Gaming is a key part of boy culture. It's how they play and socialize, so it's important to avoid demonizing video games. (You'd probably rather scroll on your phone than clean the kitchen or complete a work report, too.)

Your gaming rules and expectations should reflect your family values. Some families choose to restrict access to certain games. Some limit video game time to weekends only. Others allow unlimited access and play together as a family at nights or on weekends.

Consider your son's preferences, habits, and maturity as you establish rules. A boy who regularly goes outside to bike or work on projects in the garage needs fewer boundaries than the boys glued to a screen.

Note: There is no "right" amount of game time. You'll have to work together to create gaming guidelines, and revisit and revise them frequently as your son grows. Also be mindful of "free" games that encourage in-game purchases, as your son may inadvertently rack up a staggering credit card bill without supervision.

Phone time

By age 10, many children have their own phones. It's up to you to decide when your child is ready, but experts agree that phone ownership and usage should be considered a privilege. Do not hand your son a cell phone without establishing guidelines for use.

Initially, you should have your son's password so that you can access his phone. He should know that you'll periodically review his activities (including text messages) and that you have the right to take away his phone or restrict his phone privileges if he violates your agreed-upon expectations for behavior. Together, establish a phone contract; outline what happens if he loses his phone, exceeds data limits, or uses his phone inappropriately. (Clearly outline what you consider "inappropriate.")

Enforce two commonsense (and science-supported) rules: No phones at the dinner table (unless you've agreed in advance to share videos and memes on a particular night) and no phones in the bedroom at night. Instead, have your son plug his phone into a central charging station about an hour before bedtime.

As your son gets older and demonstrates increasing responsibility, revise your phone contract.

Social media

Social media can be great for kids; it's a way to stay in touch with friends and connect with others who share similar interests. It can also be distracting and devastating; cyberbullying often occurs via social media, and carefully curated social media feeds can cause kids to feel insecure and insignificant. In some cases, heavy use of social media has been linked to depression and eating disorders.

Completely banning your child from social media isn't an effective strategy. A better, counterintuitive option is to introduce your child to social media at a relatively young age, while your child is still open to your feedback. That's the approach used by mom Judi Ketteler, who allowed her son on Instagram at age 9. As she wrote in a *New York Times* article about their experience, her decision was "part of a deliberate strategy" to teach her children to use social media responsibly. She used some of her son's early missteps—such as posting a video of himself doing a front flip clad only in boxer shorts—to craft a set of social media rules with her son. Not sure how to handle social media? Devorah Heitner's book, *Screenwise* is packed with great tips.

YouTube/TV

Spending hours watching YouTube videos of other people playing games or riding dirt bikes may seem ridiculous to you, but remember: Adults spend a lot of time sitting on the couch watching other people play sports, too.

Most tweens turn to YouTube when they want to learn how to do something. Your son can learn all kinds of things from YouTube—including some things you'd rather he didn't. Additionally, the "suggested videos" that show up when your child chooses a video can lead down all sorts of internet rabbit holes.

You can install the YouTube Kids app to restrict and filter the content your child can access. This option may work well for younger kids; however, older boys are bound to feel frustrated by their limited access. When your son is around age 10, you may want to enable the "Restricted Mode" setting (log into YouTube, click on Settings, and choose "Restricted Mode"), which allows your son to use regular YouTube, but blocks videos that have been flagged as containing inappropriate content.

TV time is still best enjoyed as a family. Look for series you can stream together.

UNPLUGGED ACTIVITIES

Board games. Math, reading, critical thinking, problem solving, taking turns—what's not to love?

Box building. Challenge your son to build a structure or invention from empty boxes and recycled materials. He'll exercise his creativity and problem-solving skills.

Citizen scientist. Both NASA (the National Aeronautics and Space Administration) and National Geographic offer citizen scientist programs that allow boys to contribute scientific data, based on local observations.

Constructive destruction! Got an old appliance that has stopped working? Let your son dismantle it and learn a bit about electronics.

Cooking and baking. Boys can strengthen math, reading, and science skills while learning to feed themselves.

Fishing. Time in nature plus patience. And if he really wants to catch fish, your son will end up learning a lot of science as well.

Sculpting. Whether your son uses clay, metal, wood, or recycled materials, he'll strengthen his creativity, problem-solving, and visual-spatial skills.

FOR YOUR REFLECTION

1. How will you help your son connect his interests to school?
2. How will you support your son's out-of-school learning?
3. What motivates your son?
4. Are your current screen time guidelines working for your family? How can you tweak your guidelines to decrease conflict and increase cooperation?

CHAPTER SIX

Supporting Physical and Sexual Health

Your son will grow many inches over the coming years, and his body will begin its transformation to adulthood. At the same time, his burgeoning sense of independence means that you have less control over his eating, sleeping, and socializing than ever before.

It's time to start teaching your son how to respect and care for his body (and others').

Balancing Diet

First things first: Tween boys eat a lot. More than you think they need.

Most boys hit the hungry-all-the-time phase around age 10 or 11—which not so coincidentally coincides with the start of puberty and a series of growth spurts that will likely result in your son towering over you well before he turns 18.

Don't try to limit his nutritional intake. Instead, buy healthy foods and involve your son in shopping, meal planning, and cooking. Challenge him to try one new food a week (or month, depending on his adventurousness). Ask him to find recipes online that incorporate his favorite flavors and have him work together with whoever normally makes dinner to prepare them.

Snacking at school

According to the CDC, students consume about half of their daily calories at school. Since the 2014–2015 school year, all foods and beverages available at school must meet Smart Snacks in School nutrition standards, which include limits on fat, sugar, sodium, and calorie content. As a result, most students don't have easy access to soda, chips, or sweets during the school day.

However, at least one study has shown that kids' diets didn't noticeably improve after the introduction of Smart Snacks standards, as kids can still bring snacks from home, such as prepackaged chips, cookies, and crackers. You can boost your son's school-day nutrition by buying easy-to-pack healthy snacks, such as bananas, apples, nut and raisin trail mixes, low-fat yogurt, and baby carrots with dip.

Meeting nutrition requirements

In early adolescence, boys need an average of 2,800 calories a day. (Boys who play sports may need significantly more.) According to the American Academy of Pediatrics, nutritionists recommend that 50 to 60 percent of their calories should come from complex carbohydrates—foods such as whole-grain bread, brown rice, oatmeal, potatoes, corn, black beans, lentils, and chickpeas. Fat should account for no more than 30 percent of boys' calories; intake of foods high in saturated fat (beef, cheese, pork, butter) should be limited.

Don't worry about your son's protein intake. Most American tweens and teens eat twice as much protein as they need. Vegans can easily meet their protein needs by eating nuts, seeds, beans, and tofu. Resist requests for protein powder or protein supplements; these products are not regulated by the US Food and Drug Administration (FDA) and young athletes do not need them to perform well.

Your son needs calcium and vitamin D (for strong bones and teeth), vitamin A (for healthy skin), vitamin C (so that his immune system works well, and injuries heal quickly), and vitamin B (for overall health). It's best to get these nutrients from food, but if you're concerned about your son's nutritional intake, you can give him a daily multivitamin. Look for one that contains at least 600 international units (IU) of vitamin D.

Exercise

The CDC recommends that children ages 6 to 17 engage in at least 60 minutes of moderate to moderate/vigorous physical activity every day. Unfortunately, only about 24 percent of US children hit that target. Kids with physical and emotional challenges, including autism spectrum disorder, are even less likely to reach that goal.

The deck is stacked against you (and your boy): Phys-ed classes are less common in school than they once were, and much of boys' socialization and learning now occurs online. Additionally, many families lack access to safe outdoor spaces.

You can increase the likelihood that your son will engage in regular physical activity by maintaining an active lifestyle. Do not nag your son to "go outside" or "get moving" if you rarely do. Instead, go for a walk each day after supper; invite your son. Explore a local bike trail on the weekend—and insist that your son come along. (Yes, he might complain. Insist anyway and promise that he can do his preferred hobby when you get home.)

Sports and activities

Sports, of course, are a great way to build physical and emotional strength. According to Stanford Children's Health and Project Play, kids who participate in physical activity generally have improved mental health. They're also more likely to do well in school and to remain physically active later in life.

Note: Your son doesn't have to join an expensive travel team to get athletic opportunities. Look for local recreational clubs. Some city rec departments host low-cost sports leagues, as do some YMCAs. You can often find secondhand gear, as most boys this age can only use athletic gear for one season before they need a larger size.

Pay attention to the coaching. Many parents look for coaches who will hone their sons' skills but watch the coaches' language as well. Stay away from coaches who belittle and shame players, and run away from those who tell injured boys to "man up" or "rub some dirt on it and get back in there!"

Alternatives to team sports

Most young athletes choose well-known team sports, such as football, soccer, hockey, baseball, basketball, and lacrosse. Boys who enjoy physical activity but don't like team sports may enjoy swimming, tennis, karate, rock climbing, parkour, mountain biking, hiking, golf, rollerblading, ice-skating, snowboarding or skiing, or backyard trampoline. Seemingly sedentary sports, like motocross, snowmobiling, and ATV (all-terrain vehicle) riding are another option—and much more physical than they look! (Core and leg muscles get a real workout.)

Dance is an excellent physical and creative outlet. Boys who are interested in dance may need some additional support and nudging, though. Despite evolving gender norms, there's still a pretty strong social stigma against boys who dance. You can help your son by proudly supporting his interest and enrolling him in dance classes with other boys.

Daily life also includes myriad opportunities for exercise. Walking or biking to school counts as physical activity. So do gardening, wood chopping, snow shoveling, and playing outside with friends.

Nathan quit baseball when he was 11 years old. He'd gotten hit in the face with a pitch one too many times.

His basketball days were over, too. Though he played when he was younger, Nathan never really felt any passion for the game.

He was passionate about business, though, and started a lawn mowing service. Soon, he was spending hours each week mowing lawns and performing yard work for clients. In the winter, he expanded his business to include snow shoveling.

At age 12, Nathan joined his school's show choir, a competitive singing and dancing troupe. The boy who had asked for dance lessons at age 4 found his home. He honed his singing and dancing skills over the next six years, often practicing for hours a day. Show choir competitions—day-long events featuring troupes from area schools—gave him the opportunity to perform in front of crowds and improve.

As one of only a few boys in his school's show choir, Nathan faced some ridicule from his sports-loving peers. In show choir, though, he found friends who shared his interests and his talents, and his self-confidence blossomed. By senior year, he had won numerous Best Male Soloist awards and helped his group snag a Grand Champion trophy.

He continued his lawn mowing and snow shoveling business through high school as well—and when the time came to choose a college major, he combined his interests. Nathan moved to Nashville to pursue an education (and career) in the music business.

Getting Enough Sleep

According to the National Sleep Foundation, children ages 6 to 12 should get nine to eleven hours of sleep a night; the CDC recommends nine to twelve hours nightly. However, 60 percent of middle schoolers do not get enough sleep, which increases their risk of obesity, anxiety, depression, injuries, and attention and behavioral issues.

Digital distractions are a major contributor to lack of sleep. Most preteen boys would much rather scroll through social media, play video games, or watch YouTube videos than sleep. Additionally, puberty can disrupt boys' sleep schedules. Their internal body clock shifts as they enter adolescence, making it difficult for them to fall asleep at an early hour. Their body wants to stay up later and sleep later—an impossibility for many, given school start times.

Your son's sleep habits will change over the coming years, but his need for restful, restorative sleep will not.

Teaching healthy sleep habits

You can't control the onset of puberty, but you can help your son develop healthy sleep habits. Insist that he power down digital devices at least one hour before bedtime. Keep cell phones, computers, TVs, and video games out of the bedroom. (Buy your son an alarm clock so that he doesn't have to use his phone alarm. If he likes to listen to music as he falls asleep, invest in a pair of Bluetooth headphones so that he can stream music from a device located in another room.)

Set a good example by turning off your phone well before bedtime and prioritizing sleep.

Adequate physical activity and exposure to daytime sunlight also promote sleep. Make sure you and your son both spend time outside every day.

Hygiene

Tween boys are notoriously neglectful of personal hygiene. Before puberty, they don't much care about how they look (or smell). Given the choice between a shower or a few more minutes video gaming—well, most boys choose the game.

Unfortunately, a boy's body starts changing before his mind. You'll probably notice BO before your son does and it'll be up to you to tactfully introduce the idea of regular hygiene.

Showering

Up until about age 11, most boys need a bath or a shower only once or twice a week, according to the American Academy of Dermatology. Once puberty hits—and, remember, it can begin as early as age 9—they should bathe or shower daily. Work with your son to establish a regular routine. If he's groggy in the morning, let him wash up at night. (Pro tip: You might have more luck getting him to shower right after supper, especially if he's allowed to do something he enjoys after he's done.)

Men's body wash doesn't clean any better (or worse) than bar soap or gender-neutral body wash. But if your son is resisting showering, let him pick out his own shampoo and body wash. One experienced boy mom recommends buying colored body wash or soap, so your son can see which parts of his body he's washed, and which have yet to be touched.

Grooming

Don't fight with your son regarding his hairstyle or clothing. Yes, you want him to look well-groomed when he leaves the house, but your son's appearance is his business, and his mismatched, stained, or slightly too-small clothing are not a reflection of your parenting prowess.

If your son isn't interested in combing or brushing his hair, ask a stylist to help him figure out a low-maintenance cut and style.

Hold the line on toothbrushing. Oral hygiene affects overall health, so insist on twice-a-day brushing. Let him pick out his toothbrush and toothpaste. (Buying a Bluetooth-connected toothbrush might be worthwhile if he'll use it.)

Deodorant, cologne, body spray

Most boys begin using deodorant between ages 9 and 14. You'll know it's time when your son's odor lingers after he's left the room. Tween boys don't need specially formulated deodorant; regular adult preparations are fine, but you can buy natural or tween-focused products, if you prefer.

Believe it or not, boys' sense of smell is generally not as acute as adult women's, so your son might not be lying when he tells you he smells "just fine!" Tween boys' lack of scent sensitivity may be why they tend to go overboard when they discover cologne and body spray.

Honoring Sexuality

Sex is an integral part of human life.

It can be really uncomfortable to think of your son as a sexual being, and downright scary to realize that you (and the men in his life) will have to talk to him about puberty, porn, sex, and consent. After all, the truth is that we adults still have a lot to learn, even if we've been having sex for years. Many of us still carry around sexual shame and guilt, and a history of scary or less-than-satisfying sexual experiences. Preparing our sons for healthy sexual relationships can seem a bit beyond our capability because we're still figuring it out ourselves.

Breathe.

You are absolutely capable of giving your son accurate information and conveying positive messages about human sexuality. Talking about sex while your son is young is actually easier than waiting until he's in his teens, as he's more open to your input before adolescence.

Some children go through puberty earlier than others. Some are eager to engage in sexual activity; others would rather wait. In either case, it is better to provide information sooner rather than later.

Talking about sex and sexuality won't encourage your child to have sex. On the contrary: Children whose parents discuss sex, relationships, and family values with them are more likely to delay sex. Avoiding discussions of sex and sexuality conveys the message that sex is shameful and may cause boys to seek advice elsewhere.

Why not redirect some of the energy you're currently expending worrying about your son's grades into teaching him about relationships? As Amy Lang, sex education expert and author of *Bird + Bees + Your Kids: A Guide to Sharing Your Beliefs about Sexuality, Love and Relationships,* says, "It's way more important to be sexually savvy and understand healthy relationships than to score a 9,000 on the PSAT."

Puberty

Your son might learn a bit about puberty at school or via conversations with his doctor, but he'll probably need more info. You might need to learn a little, too. Here are the basics.

Some boys begin puberty as early as 8; others, as late as 16. This wide variation can cause great distress. Looking like you're 8 when you're really 12 can be tough on a boy's self-esteem and social standing, especially if he has peers who look like they're 16. Unfortunately, there's nothing you or your son can do to rush puberty. (However, if your son hasn't shown any signs of puberty by age 14, consult a doctor.)

You probably won't notice the first physical signs of puberty—enlargement of the testicles and sprouting pubic hair. Make sure your son knows that these changes are completely normal. Next is usually a growth spurt. You might notice your son's increased appetite first. Physical growth can be uneven; a boy's hands and feet often grow before the rest of his body (which is one reason that young teenagers are often clumsy). Boys can grow as much as two to three inches (or more!) in a year. They also add muscle, and their shoulders broaden as their jawline becomes more pronounced.

Boys' voices begin changing and some boys' voices seem to change nearly overnight. Other boys go through months of unpredictable vocal changes.

The hormonal changes of puberty cause increased sweating, body odor, and acne. Regular showers and face washing help with all three of these issues. (A doctor can help with persistent sweating, body odor, or acne.)

Boys' penises grow during puberty as well, and between ages 11 and 15, most boys experience their first ejaculation, either during masturbation or while sleeping.

Masturbation

Little boys commonly touch their penis—it's an easily accessible part of the body and touching it feels good. According to the American Academy of Pediatrics, "Up to the age of five or six years, masturbation is quite common."

Masturbation usually tapers off during the elementary school years and resumes when puberty triggers sexual thoughts and curiosity about the sexual functioning of the body. It is totally normal for tween boys to masturbate. In fact, a 2009 survey of 800 teenagers revealed that three-quarters of boys report masturbating; half said they masturbated at least twice a week.

Contrary to what some of us were told as children, masturbation does not cause blindness, pimples, or warts, and it is not linked to promiscuity. If you accidentally walk in on your son masturbating, quickly apologize ("I'm so sorry") and leave the room, closing the door behind you. Try not to gasp or react with shock. Later, you can apologize again: "I'm sorry about before. That was awkward. Next time, make sure the door is closed/locked, and I'll be sure to knock." Keeping your tone calm will reassure your son that he's done nothing wrong.

Porn and explicit content

By age 11, most boys have found online pornography. Curiosity about sex and bodies is part of puberty, so many boys search online for "sex" and "boobs." Those developmentally appropriate searches can lead to graphic content.

Sex educator Amy Lang advises parents to install (and use) both parental controls and monitoring. Devices such as Circle allow you to filter internet access on every device in your home, which can go a long way toward limiting your son's access and exposure to porn. Parental monitoring apps, such as Bark, scan your child's social media, texts, emails, and website history and alert you to potential issues, so you can talk about them with your child.

Your son needs to know that porn and sex are two different things. Lang recommends saying something like this: "Wanting to learn more about sex is totally natural and normal. Sometimes kids will look at porn on the internet because they are curious or find it exciting. Porn is not real sex—it's someone's fantasy about what sex could be like."

You also have to discuss sexting. According to a 2019 study by the parenting app Jiminy, an estimated one in ten kids is exposed to a sexually explicit message by age 8. Be clear: Tweens should never send or ask for nude pictures.

CONVERSATION STARTERS

→ "I want you to know that I'm installing some internet filters. It's totally normal to be interested in and curious about sex and the human body, but I want to make sure you're getting good information . . ."

→ "What would you do if someone asked you for a naked picture?"

→ "How do you think you'll know if someone wants to kiss you?"

→ "I read that a lot of kids see porn before they're 12 years old. How many of your friends do you think have seen porn?"

LGBTQIA Support

Approximately 5 percent of Americans self-identify as lesbian, gay, bisexual, or transgender, according to a 2020 Gallop poll.

You can't assume that your son is straight. Or gay. Or male. Over the past 25 years, it's become increasingly apparent that making assumptions about a person's gender or sexuality may be hurtful, harmful, and wrong.

That statement may seem jarring to many of us parents, who grew up in a time and place where people were categorized as male or female, and boys had girlfriends and girls had boyfriends. The term *transgender* wasn't part of common language, and same-sex marriage wasn't legal.

Today, society acknowledges the broad spectrum of gender and sexuality. Many of today's kids are more comfortable with current terminology than their parents are, so let's break it down. LGBTQIA = lesbian, gay, bisexual, transgender, queer, intersex, and asexual.

+ Lesbian: a woman who is sexually attracted to women.

+ Gay: a person who's sexually attracted to a person of the same gender.

+ Bisexual: a person who's attracted to people of the same and other genders.

+ Transgender: a person who does not identify with the gender they were assigned at birth. A person who is born with a penis and called a "boy" at birth may be a trans woman.

+ Queer: once used as a derogatory term, *queer* has been adopted by members of the LGBTQIA community to describe a person who is not heterosexual or does not identify with the gender they were assigned at birth.

+ Intersex: a person who has reproductive or sexual anatomy that doesn't seem to fit the typical definition of female or male.

+ Asexual: a person who experiences little to no sexual attraction.

Despite recent societal shifts, many people still assume that little boys will develop crushes on girls and grow up to be men. Parents and grandparents often ask tween boys if they "have a girlfriend yet." A boy who's beginning to realize that he's physically attracted to other boys may feel embarrassed or ashamed by a such a question and conclude that there's something wrong with his attraction—or with him.

Encouraging conversations

You love your son.

He needs to know that you will always love him, unconditionally.

Making a few subtle shifts in your language can help you avoid saying anything that could unintentionally alienate your son. For example, instead of asking, "Do you have a girlfriend?" try "Do you have a crush on anyone?" Using gender-neutral language conveys openness and acceptance.

Right now, it's important to demonstrate openness and acceptance. Treat all people you encounter with respect. Educate yourself about gender and sexuality. (Amaze.org is a great resource.)

Responding supportively

If your son confides in you and shares information about his sexual identity or gender, you can say:

+ "Thanks for telling me. It means a lot to me that you trusted me with this information."

+ "I love you. I will always love you."

+ "How can I support you?"

+ "Is this just between you and me right now, or does anyone else know this?"

+ "Do you want to talk about this some more?"

Dating

Do you remember your first crush? Who your best friend liked when you were both in fifth grade?

Your son may seem too young for romance, but if you're honest with yourself, you probably started seeing your classmates in a different light around age 10 or 11. By fifth grade, many kids are interested in romantic relationships. Crushes are common, and so are special relationships between tweens who like each other.

These early relationships are important, as they give young people a chance to build their communication skills and experiment with giving and receiving affection. It will likely be many years before your son is ready to date, but his romantic interests now aren't unimportant. Don't dismiss or belittle his crushes or relationships. Instead, talk to your son about healthy relationships and share your family values regarding dating.

Note: Because girls typically begin puberty about two years before boys, they may be interested in romantic relationships well before their male peers. And because we live in a highly sexualized culture and kids emulate what they see, some boys report intense sexual pressure from girls their age. According to a 2005 study, published in 2010 in *Perspectives on Sexual and Reproductive Health*, as many as 8 percent of surveyed middle school students engaged in oral sex before the end of eighth grade. A 2014 study, published in *Psychology of Men & Masculinity*, found that a quarter of high school and college-aged young men surveyed experienced coercion by seduction; nearly one-third were verbally coerced into sexual activity.

Your son needs to know that it's okay to say no and that sex is not a requirement to "be a man." Give him some stock excuses he can use to get out of sticky situations: "I don't want that on my phone," "I gotta go. My mom will be crazy if I'm not home in 10 minutes," "I gotta keep my strength up for the game."

Keep your eyes and ears open. Don't make any assumptions about your son's romantic life, but do ask questions. Good conversation starters include "Is anyone in your class dating someone?" or "How do kids your age let someone know they like a person?"

Sharing feelings appropriately

What tweens really want and need to know—even more than details about the mechanics of sex—is how to let someone know they like them, how to get the attention of another person, and how to move beyond friendship to romance.

We adults tend to skip that part of the conversation, and that's a mistake. Turn on the news: You'll see plenty of examples of people handling this part of life inappropriately. If you want your son to be a non-creepy good guy, it's a good idea to give him a few guidelines for sharing his feelings:

+ DO communicate directly. Having a friend tell someone you like them is a time-honored practice, but a lot can go wrong if you do that.

+ DO share what you like about them. Let your son know that it's a good idea to focus on nonphysical attributes: "I really like talking to you" is a better option than "You have sexy eyes."

+ DON'T lead with physical suggestions. "I want to kiss you all over" is not a good opening line.

Responding to rejection

Your son's ability to handle rejection and frustration is more important than you may realize. You've been helping him develop his emotional intelligence and resilience ever since he was little; now it's time to help him apply those skills to romantic and social rejection.

Step 1: Empathize with him. Rejection hurts. Acknowledge that pain, and allow him time to feel it, rather than saying something like "There are other fish in the sea!"

Step 2: Remind him that all humans have the right to make personal decisions. And that being with someone who *wants* to be with you is much more fun than being with someone who's not into you.

Step 3: Distract and redirect. Help your son identify and focus on the positive things in his life. Encourage him to spend his time on his personal interests, rather than pining after someone who doesn't currently want to be with him. If he's open to it, you can suggest some activities to help him process his pain. (Good options include physical activity, listening to music, journaling, or making art.) If he's not open to suggestions, back off and give him time.

Being respectful online

Because so much socialization now occurs online, it's essential for you to outline your expectations for online behavior. Your son needs to know that you will not tolerate disrespectful or bullying behavior online.

You'll have to explicitly detail which behaviors are (and are not) allowed. Allowed: Talking and joking with real-life friends. Discussing homework and events. Making plans. Sharing creations and ideas. Not allowed: Derogatory comments or racial, ethnic, or sexist slurs. Threatening physical or emotional violence. Bullying. Sending or receiving nude or sexually provocative images. Sexting.

You will have to repeat these expectations over and over again, and it's almost certain that your son will violate one (or more) of your rules. A few mistakes do not mean that your son is destined to become an internet troll. However, you should clearly define and apply consequences when needed, such as loss of cell phone/internet/video game time or reading (or writing) a research paper or making a presentation on the harms of sexting/trolling/cyberbullying.

How to talk about consent

Consent isn't all (or only) about sex. Consent is really about acknowledging and respecting other people's boundaries.

By age 8, your son should know that no one is allowed to touch him unless he says it's okay. If you haven't yet had that talk with your son, have it ASAP—and make sure he knows that he shouldn't touch other people without their consent, either. The notion of consent gets a little tricky in boy world because preteen boys often "initiate conversation" by playfully touching one another; a shove, a fist bump, a high five, or a gentle punch on the shoulder can be an invitation to play.

Teach your son to monitor other people's faces and body language. Signs of discomfort include pulling away or frowning; all physical play should stop immediately if any of these signs are present. Smiles, laughing, or a return touch may be signs of consent, but teach your son to check in verbally, too, rather than assuming consent. Among friends, a simple comment like "You wanna play?" will often suffice. As your son gets older, you can expand the conversation to the need for verbal check-ins during sexual situations.

FOR YOUR REFLECTION

1. What physical activities do you and your son both enjoy? What would you like to try?
2. Is your son currently getting enough sleep? How will you help him establish a healthy sleep schedule?
3. When do you think kids should be allowed to date?

PART THREE

Between Your Son and the World

When your son was little, you could protect him from most of life's hardships. As he gets older, it becomes more difficult—and, frankly, undesirable—to shelter him from challenges. Tweens are increasingly aware of the world around them. They pick up on stress at home and in the community, and may experience sexism, racism, and violence.

Your son will look to you for guidance, answers, and support. You can introduce nuance and context into conversations about global issues, and you can help your son identify positive actions he can take, even now, to make the world a better place.

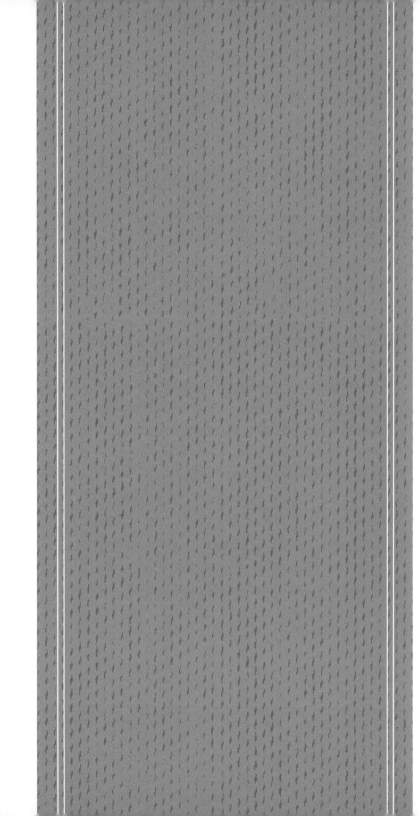

CHAPTER SEVEN

Navigating Tough Times

Life is often less than perfect.

You and your son will almost certainly encounter some serious challenges in the years ahead. Some you may be able to predict and prepare for; others will drop into your lives suddenly.

No one wants to go through tough times, but they're a constant of the human experience. And though we'd prefer to avoid pain, we often learn and grow through adversity.

You can't shield your son from tragedy or misfortune, but you can support him, love him, and teach him the skills he'll need to survive life's inevitable setbacks.

Moving

Moving to a new town or school can be stressful and scary. The tween/ teen years are all about fitting in, and it can be devastating for a child to have to leave a group of close-knit friends. Saying goodbye to a familiar school can trigger anxiety and sadness; moving also creates upheaval in a child's extracurricular activities. A boy who's developed a reputation as a shortstop, for instance, knows he'll have to prove himself all over again when he goes out for baseball in a new place.

However, you can't assume that your son will be upset by an impending move. Some boys—especially boys who feel misunderstood by their peers and teachers—may welcome an opportunity to start over, unimpeded by their previous reputation.

Inform your son of the move as soon as possible and give him space and time to explore his emotions. If, in a burst of anger, he says, "Why do we have to move anyway? Moving sucks!" don't launch into a litany of the likely benefits of your move or say something trite like, "It'll be fine. I'm sure you'll make lots of friends." Instead, empathize with him: "Yeah. Moving can be tough."

If you can, bring your son along to tour potential homes and schools, and consider his input and feedback. Allow him to pack (or help pack) and unpack his own belongings.

Social media makes it easy for kids to stay connected despite geographic distance. Support your son's efforts to stay in touch with friends from "home," even as you encourage him to make new ones. You could, for example, tell your son you'll give him some extra screen time to game with old friends after he checks out a new club or extracurricular activity.

Divorce, Separation, and Relationship Conflict

More than half of all US children don't live with two parents who are married for the first time. Most do just fine despite their parents' relationship status.

Although divorce, separation, and relationship conflict can be traumatizing for children of all ages, research has shown that children can thrive in all kinds of families: Married. Single parent. Divorced. In fact, the marital status of the parents matters less to a child's overall health and well-being than economic stability and psychological safety. Divorce or separation does not doom your child; studies have found very few differences in academic achievement, mental health, behavior, and the ability to form close relationships between children of divorced or unmarried parents and children whose parents remained together.

However, it's difficult to overestimate the disruptive effect of a divorce or separation. A change in parental relationships often triggers changes in living environment, economic status, and family routines. If one parent moves away, the loss of daily or regular interaction can feel like abandonment to a young boy.

Shared parenting can minimize the potentially negative impact of a divorce or separation. Studies have shown that children who spend at least 35 percent of their time with each parent do better academically, socially, and psychologically than those who don't.

Discussing relationship problems

Telling your son about your relationship problems may be one of the most difficult things you ever do. However, keep in mind that your son may already be aware of tension within your relationship.

Choose a calm, comfortable time and place—and be flexible. If your son comes home from school upset about a test, you may want to delay your talk until another time.

If possible, both parents should participate in the conversation. Be matter-of-fact. If appropriate, you can say something like this: "As you probably know, we've been fighting a lot lately/not getting along." Then, tell your son what comes next ("We're going to spend some time apart/ We're getting a divorce/etc."). If your son bolts from the room, give him time before resuming your conversation. Some kids need just a few minutes alone; others may need a few hours to process your news.

Do not blame either parent; kids don't need to know who had an affair or who decided to call it quits. Emphasize your shared love for your son and reassure him that he did not cause or contribute to your relationship problems. Describe what will happen next, including who will live where, when your son will see each parent, and who will take him to and from school and extracurricular activities.

Avoiding parentification

Do not confide in your son or share details about your relationship. Your son is also lonely, hurt, scared, and angry, and pouring out your pain will only add to his.

You may feel utterly lost and confused, but your son needs to know that you're handling things and will take care of him.

It's okay if your son sees you crying and offers you a tissue and a hug. However, if you regularly turn to your son for comfort, he may feel that he must suppress his own emotions so that he can care for you (see "Parentification" on page 23).

Similarly, it's all right if your son needs to take on a few extra responsibilities, such as folding laundry or cleaning the bathroom. It's not okay to expect your son to handle all the chores once done by the other parent.

Taking care of your own emotional needs is the best way to avoid parentification. Schedule phone calls and chats with friends. Go for walks or process your feelings via journaling. Work with a therapist, if necessary.

Minimizing disruptions to routine

Maintaining as many family routines as possible can help your son feel safe and secure. Continue morning, homework, meal, and bedtime routines, adapting them as necessary. If his other parent normally tucked him into bed each night, you may now have to do so at least a few nights a week, but you can keep a consistent bedtime and order of operations. (Brush teeth, play or read together, quiet time in the bedroom, then lights out, for instance.)

Enforcing similar family rules at both parents' houses may be helpful; however, it's possible to raise well-adjusted children even if parents have different rules regarding bedtime, homework, and screen time.

If your son will be splitting his time between two homes, do your best to maintain a regular schedule (Monday and Tuesday with Dad, Wednesday/Thursday with Mom, alternate weekends, for instance) so that your son knows what to expect. Allow flexibility to accommodate unexpected opportunities, however. If your son's dad snags tickets to a Chicago Bulls game, let your basketball-loving son go, even if the game falls on "your" night.

Depending on your relationship, you may be able to celebrate holidays and special occasions together as a family. If you can set your differences aside, your son may appreciate continuation of family traditions.

Helping him cope

Like you, your son will likely experience a myriad of emotions, including sadness, anger, disappointment, and grief. And, also like you, he'll probably wonder what happened. He'll replay memories in his mind, searching for clues, and he may hope for eventual family reunification.

Give your son opportunities to talk to you, but don't be surprised if he merely grunts when you ask him how he's doing. Remember: Many tween boys have internalized the idea that showing feelings is akin to weakness, and boys are generally less likely to process their feelings via conversation.

Watch for bursts of anger and irritation; boys frequently express sadness, fear, and frustration in angry, out-of-proportion flare-ups. A boy who punches a hole in the wall after learning that he can't have his preferred birthday cake this year may be more upset about the fact that both his parents won't be at his party than he is about the cake. Give him time to cool down; then, go talk to him. (You can say something like, "Wow. I've never seen you so upset about cake before. What's going on?")

Some boys benefit from counseling sessions with a therapist, but many do not. If your son is resistant to therapy, save your money; forcing a child to attend therapy sessions is rarely productive. However, if you notice drastic changes in your son's behavior (loss of interest in activities he normally enjoys, withdrawal from friends), consult a health-care provider or mental health professional.

Alcohol, Substance Use, and Addiction in the Family

Nearly nine million American children live with at least one parent who has a substance use disorder, according to data from National Surveys on Drug Use and Health. One in 10 kids lives with a parent who has an alcohol use disorder; 1 in 35 lives with an adult who used illicit drugs over the past year.

Studies have consistently shown that children who live with an alcoholic or addicted parent are more likely than other children to develop mental health and behavioral problems, including anxiety, depression, and conduct disorders, which are marked by hostile and physically violent behavior. Children of alcoholics and addicts are at increased risk of developing a substance use disorder later in life.

However, more than half of children of addicted parents do *not* abuse alcohol or drugs. Having at least one sober parent (or parental figure) can mitigate the impact of a substance use disorder on a child.

Feeling conflicted, confused, and distrustful

Living with an adult whose behavior is occasionally (or often) altered by substances can be scary and confusing. Children may become hyper-independent because they can't count on their parent to consistently care for them. In some cases, children end up caring for their parents or younger siblings. Boys who've had to take on adult responsibilities at young ages often grow into men who have a hard time trusting other people.

Children of alcoholic and addicted parents may struggle with conflicting feelings of love, hate, concern, and loathing because the same person can be caring and attentive sometimes and loud, scary, or abusive at other times.

Acknowledge your son's feelings. Let him know that it's possible to both love and dislike the same individual. It may be a good idea to schedule some therapy appointments for your son; a professional can help him process his complex emotions.

Having low self-esteem and self-consciousness

Tweens are egocentric. Developmentally, they're prone to assuming that others' behavior is a response to them. It is quite common for children of alcoholic or addicted parents to think they are somehow responsible—if they were better behaved or earned better grades, their parent wouldn't turn to drugs or alcohol. This misplaced sense of responsibility can fuel feelings of low self-esteem and failure.

Tweens are also easily embarrassed. A child growing up with a parent who uses substances may be very reluctant to invite friends over and may take extreme measures (such as lying about the date or time of his basketball game, for instance) to keep his parent from interacting with his peers or their parents.

Respect your son's boundaries—even if that means facilitating away-from-home playdates (at a local park, for instance) or dropping him off a block away from school. Bolster his self-esteem by naming and acknowledging his special talents and skills ("You manage to make other people feel loved" or "You are so good with animals").

Overachieving and perfectionism

In some cases, a child's desire to avoid creating additional chaos in the family morphs into unhealthy perfectionism and overachievement. The child may unconsciously think that if he does everything right, everything will be fine at home.

Alternatively, a son who is striving hard for good grades—and is devasted when he receives a B+ on a test—may be quietly terrified that he'll turn into a "drunk" or a "failure" later in life. Acknowledge your son's desire for excellence but remind him that mistakes are part of life. Reassure him that he did not cause and is not responsible for the issues in your family.

Organizations such as Al-Anon and Alateen can help you and your son cope with alcoholism or substance use.

Mental Health Issues in the Family

About one in five children in the United States lives with a parent who has severe depression.

Uncontrolled mental illness can impact every individual in a family. Adults who struggle with anxiety and depression, for instance, may have a difficult time forming close connections with their children. Untreated anxiety, depression, and bipolar disorder can even lead to neglect and abuse. Some studies have found that children of parents with mental illness are more likely to develop behavior problems, less likely to do well in school, and may have their physical health compromised.

However, parents with well-managed mental health issues are just as likely to raise well-adjusted children as parents without mental health challenges.

If you have depression, anxiety, post-traumatic stress disorder (PTSD), or any other mental health disorder, seeking professional assistance and treatment is the best thing you can do for yourself *and* your son. Health-care professionals can help you control your symptoms, which will allow you to provide a more consistent and stable environment for your son.

If another member of the family has a mental health disorder, your steady presence in your son's life will provide a measure of protection. Your son may need you to explain mental illness to him; without an explanation for his loved one's actions, your son may assume that he's the cause of this erratic or distant behavior. The website Children of Parents with a Mental Illness (see "Resources," page 150) is packed with helpful information.

Family or individual counseling can also help a child cope with mental illness in the family. Your child's pediatrician or school counselor may be able to recommend a therapist.

Economic Anxiety

Lack of money affects family well-being.

According to the American Psychological Association, socioeconomic status is "a consistent and reliable predictor of a vast array of outcomes across the life span, including physical and psychological health." Families with few financial resources generally face far more stressors and this exposure to chronic stress creates additional anxiety.

Preteens are acutely aware of socioeconomic differences. Your son may feel great pressure to wear the "right" sneakers, and you may feel great distress at your inability to provide them—as well as frustration and anger directed at your son for wanting such a thing when it's hard enough to get food on the table.

There are no easy or quick answers to economic disparity. Systemic issues beyond your control affect your family's financial situation and that's a difficult concept to explain to a tween. However, you can talk in generalities: "Some families start out with a lot of money; others do not. Unlucky breaks, such as a house fire, a job layoff, or a serious illness can devastate a family. The amount of money a person has is not a measure of his worth."

Sharing some basic information about the costs of living with your son will build his financial literacy and help him understand why some purchases are priorities and others are not. If your son asks for a high-priced item that's beyond your budget, you can:

Empathize with him. "Yeah, that would be cool, wouldn't it?"

Crunch some numbers. Together, add up the cost of housing, food, health care, and transportation. He may be shocked by how little is left.

Explore alternatives. Is a used, secondhand, or refurbished version of the item available? Could he earn some money and save up to purchase it in the future? Barter with a friend?

Illness and Death

Few things in life are as difficult as losing a loved one.

Perhaps the most challenging thing about explaining illness and death to our children is that we don't understand it ourselves. We don't know why some people get sick or die young while others thrive; there are no satisfactory answers.

Unlike younger children, preteens understand that serious illness can lead to death and that death is permanent. However, they may still harbor some inaccurate beliefs, such as thinking that their behavior somehow caused or contributed to their loved one's sickness and death. And, like younger kids, tweens sometimes regress when they experience loss. A boy who's been steadily pulling away from his family may suddenly become your shadow or refuse to walk to school alone. Alternatively, some tween boys pull even further away from family and friends. They may rebuke all attempts at conversation and soldier on as if nothing has changed.

Helping your son process his grief is particularly challenging because you're probably grieving, too. You may want nothing more than to tuck yourself in bed for the next three days (or months)—but your son is clamoring for your attention. Or you might be ready to talk and your son insists he's "fine." Give each other grace. All humans grieve differently.

Asad's dad died suddenly just a few days after he turned 13.

In the days that followed, Asad "cried a lot and rarely got out of bed," says Nadeem, his mother. "He kept the room dark and only talked to me. I was too deep in my own grief to really do anything. I simply stayed with him in the dark room."

Over the next few months, Nadeem noticed that her son would stop talking if he heard her crying. "I tried my best not to cry in his presence," she says, "but he can read me well. He went out of his way to try to make me talk about my feelings, too."

Midnight talks helped Nadeem and Asad process their grief. "We talk about the meaning of life, death, and what there may be after death," Nadeem says. "I think listening to him express himself has been really helpful. I didn't try to give any advice because, honestly, there's nothing to say. We just talk about how we feel."

Approximately four months after their loss, Nadeem took Asad to see a counselor. The boy was reluctant. "It took the therapist a long time to get anything out of him, but once he opened up, he was happier and more talkative," Nadeem says.

Answering difficult questions

Illness and death bring up a lot of difficult questions, including:

Will I get sick and die? Will you? Your son needs your help to put current events into perspective. Give him the facts: "Everyone dies eventually, but we're both likely going to be here for a long time." If your loved one has a contagious illness, emphasize measures you're taking to protect your son: "Grandma has COVID, but remember all the steps we've taken to stay safe? We're going to keep wearing our masks and washing our hands, and we'll keep our distance while she's sick."

What's it like to die? Your son needs help understanding the dying process. He needs to know that people tend to sleep more and eat and drink less as they approach death, but that they can usually hear those around them. Reassure him that health-care providers treat pain and keep people comfortable.

What happens after death? Your answer to this question will depend on your personal and religious beliefs. However, remember that tween boys are often very literal. Your son may be looking for logistical details, so tell him about funeral or memorial plans, too.

Reinforcing agency

Support your son as he finds his own unique ways to honor his loved one.

Liam, age 10, played his violin for his grandmother while she was in hospice care. When she passed away, he withdrew from his family and friends, saying very little. His parents gave him space and time to grieve. They told him about their plans to attend her funeral together, but did not lay expectations upon him. Liam chose to wear a suit and surprised his parents by standing up and delivering a moving tribute to his grandmother at her memorial service.

Do not force your son to attend a funeral. Instead, offer to help him express his feelings of loss and grief, and remember the person in another way. (Options include looking at old photos, telling stories, lighting a candle, drawing a picture, or making a project.)

CONVERSATION STARTERS

→ "You've probably noticed that Uncle Bob isn't as strong or as active as he used to be. What do you think about that?"

→ "I know I've been spending a lot of time on the phone and at the hospital recently. Do you have any questions? I've been so busy I'm afraid I haven't made time to talk with you."

→ "How can I help you cope with everything that's going on?"

→ "What do you remember most about Grandma?"

Listening without judgment

Kids—like adults—have complex feelings. Illness and death can spur memories both good and bad, and your son needs room to express them all. Tween boys, in particular, may be frustrated by adults' tendency to focus on the positive qualities of the sick or deceased.

Practice active listening skills (see "Practicing Active Listening" on page 38). If your son says something like "I hate Grandpa!" don't yell at him or become defensive. Instead, take a deep breath (or a break, if you need one) and then say something like this: "Wow. You sound really upset" or "You hate Grandpa?" Reflecting your son's words gives him time to unpack and express his feelings. The boy who "hates Grandpa" might be mad that Grandpa died before they could go on their fishing trip together.

Listening without judgment takes a lot of emotional effort, and you may be emotionally exhausted in the wake of illness and death. Care for yourself; you'll be better able to support your son if you have people who listen to you without judgment. Grief counseling or grief support groups can help parents, children, and families navigating loss.

FOR YOUR REFLECTION

1. What was your "toughest time" when you were a child? How did the adults in your life help you? How did they make things worse?
2. How do you cope with tough times? What are your son's go-to coping strategies?
3. Who can you reach out to for additional support if necessary? What support groups are available in your area?

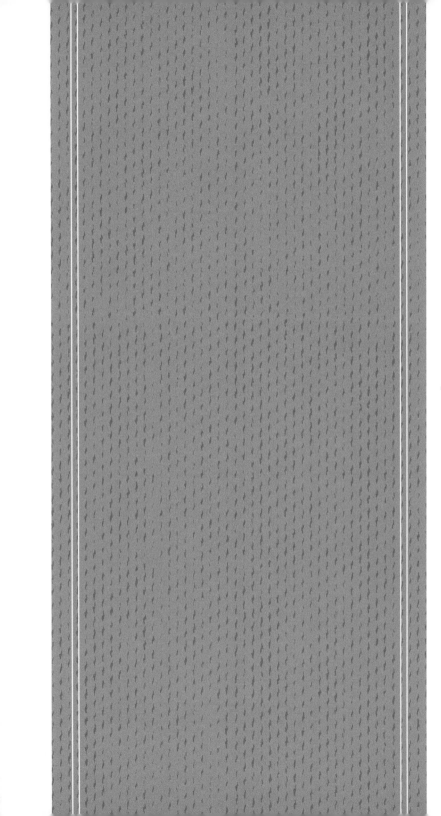

CHAPTER EIGHT

Big-Picture Conversations

As your son grows, so will his awareness of the outside world. Right now, he's still predominantly focused on himself (totally developmentally normal!), but he's becoming aware of social issues, news, and natural disasters—and wondering how they affect him and his future.

We can't protect kids from scary news, and on social media they are bombarded with headlines, sound bites, and memes that often oversimplify complex events. So, we can't avoid topics like racism, sexism, and violence. These topics affect our boys' well-being. We need to provide context, information, support, and reassurance to help them understand their place in a changing world.

Racism, Social Justice, and Equality

Racism affects nearly every aspect of boys' experience.

Black boys are more likely to be expelled or suspended from school than other students. According to a 2018 report by the Government Accountability Office, Black students account for nearly 40 percent of public school suspensions, even though they make up only 15.5 percent of the public school population.

White boys are often given a pass for their behavior. In 2018, the *Milwaukee Journal Sentinel* reported that a federal investigation of Milwaukee public schools found more than 100 instances over a two-year period in which Black students were punished more severely than white students for similar conduct.

During the COVID-19 pandemic, boys (and girls) of Asian descent reported an uptick in racial bullying. One-quarter of Asian American adults surveyed said they'd recently been the targets of racism, according to a 2020 survey.

Latino boys were taunted by classmates chanting "Build the wall!" during the 2016 and 2020 elections, and a 2011 study, published in the journal *Ethnic and Racial Studies*, found that Hispanic children were more likely than others to report that people thought that they were "not smart" because of their race.

Racism influences child development and physical and mental health, according to the American Academy of Pediatrics (AAP). The experience of racism can directly influence access to safe neighborhoods, nutritious foods, and health care, and trigger a chronic stress state in the body, which also increases the risk of chronic diseases. Racism is also linked to depression, anxiety, post-traumatic stress disorder (PTSD), and suicidal thoughts and behavior. The AAP calls racism "a socially transmitted disease passed down through generations" that has "powerful impacts . . . on health outcomes . . . and [the] well-being of children and adolescents."

Across the world, people are working to stop racism.

Recognize privilege

The concept of male privilege can be very difficult for boys to understand and accept. Tween boys know that girls are typically the academic stars in the classroom. They know women can be elected to the highest levels of government and excel on the soccer field and in the boardroom. To boys surrounded by "girl power," the idea of male privilege may seem like a cruel joke.

Similarly, white boys growing up in non-diverse communities may not recognize white skin as a built-in advantage, especially if their families face economic or other challenges. Of course, families who are raising BIPOC (Black, Indigenous, People of Color) children, particularly Black boys, know that many people are inclined to judge their sons harshly, regardless of their family's socioeconomic status.

We parents need to help our sons understand the many ways in which gender, race, and sexuality have been used to limit opportunities for some. You can help your son wrap his head around male privilege by sharing your experiences with sexism. (Did anyone ever tell you you're "too smart" for a girl? Or ask if you were married or had kids during a job interview?)

Use the "Check Your Privilege" TikTok challenge to discuss racial privilege with your son. The challenge, started by a Virginia woman who goes by @boss_bigmommma, asks people if they've ever been called a racial slur or followed unnecessarily in a store, among other things.

Discuss history makers

You and your son are probably already familiar with Martin Luther King Jr. and Rosa Parks, civil rights leaders who advocated for change. But the fight for social justice didn't end in the 1960s; it continues today. Consider including some of these history makers in your discussions with your son:

Colin Kaepernick. The former San Francisco 49s quarterback made headlines by kneeling, rather than standing, when the national anthem was played before games. Taking a knee was his way of protesting racial injustice in the United States. You can compare reaction to Kaepernick with public reactions to Martin Luther King Jr. in the 1960s. (MLK Jr., like Kaepernick, was accused of being divisive and disrespectful and most Americans rated King more negatively than positively at the time.)

Larry Kramer. In 1987, Kramer, an American author and playwright, founded ACT UP (AIDS Coalition to Unleash Power). At a time when same-sex marriage was illegal and AIDS was viewed, by some, as a punishment for homosexuality, Kramer advocated for LGBTQ+ rights.

Kamala Harris. The first female vice president in United States history, Harris, the daughter of an Indian mother and a Jamaican father, was also the first Black woman to serve as California's attorney general.

Take concrete actions

There's so much you can do to advocate for equality. It may be best to start small. Look around: What issues are problematic in your community? What efforts are already under way and how can you help? Here are some ideas:

Volunteer with and donate to local social and racial justice organizations. National organizations that may have a local chapter in your area include the NAACP, the largest civil rights organization in the United States, and the American Civil Liberties Union (ACLU). Search online for racial justice organizations to find local agencies.

Sign petitions. Color of Change, which describes itself as the country's "largest online racial justice organization," regularly shares petitions with those who sign up for updates. Kids in Need of Defense (KIND), an organization that advocates for the rights of immigrant children separated from their families, also has an online petition.

Act online. Social media can fuel revolutions. KIND suggests hashtags (#Protect Families, #KeepFamiliesTogether) you can use to amplify their efforts. Your son can help you find others.

Speak up! Whenever you hear someone using a racial slur or saying something derogatory about a group of people, speak up. Practice responses with your son. Some ideas: "That's not cool" or "Laughing at other people isn't funny."

> *Jay was in middle school when he came home with broken glasses and a scrape on his face.*
>
> *His mother, Chandra White-Cummings, was surprised; no one had contacted her to tell her Jay had been injured in a fight, even though the school had already sent her numerous emails and notes complaining about Jay's behavior.*
>
> *As Chandra worked to figure out what happened, she noticed a few disturbing details: The gym teacher asked the white boy involved in the scuffle to share his side of the story first. The benefit of the doubt went to the white child, not Jay, a Black boy—in fact, Jay's homeroom teacher punished him. When Chandra called the teacher to discuss the incident, she was informed that "Jay has a bit of a reputation."*
>
> *Chandra knows that her son isn't perfect, but she sensed racism at work. Jay told his mom the teacher was picking on him, and his feelings were soon confirmed by several white classmates, who told Chandra that "Jay gets the short end of the stick." One even said he'd done many of the same things as Jay but never gotten into trouble. Chandra realized that her son's declining grades were likely the result of the stress he was experiencing at school.*
>
> *After a less-than-satisfactory meeting with the principal, Chandra pulled Jay out of school and homeschooled him for the rest of the year. Her son initially resisted the change, but within one month he came to his mother with tears in his eyes and said, "Thank you. I feel like I can finally breathe." His grades rebounded and his love of learning returned.*

Violence

Boys are surrounded by violence. Some live in neighborhoods in which gun violence is common. Many play first-person shooter video games and nearly all have watched dozens, if not hundreds, of hours of violence in movies and on TV shows.

According to the National Survey of Children's Exposure to Violence, in 2014, nearly 25 percent of children ages 17 and younger reported witnessing violence; boys were more likely to report exposure than girls. Fifty-six percent of boys also reported being victims of violence.

Exposure to violence can harm children physically and emotionally. According to the National Institute of Justice, kids who encounter and experience violence are more likely to struggle in school, use substances, act aggressively, and develop depression or other mental health challenges.

Violence is so endemic in our society that you'll have to help your son cope with unsettling images and experiences. Here's how.

Listen

When a violent event, such as a school shooting or a murder-suicide, takes place in your community or hits the headlines, don't ignore the topic. Thanks to social media and online news, kids may even see disturbing images online before they come home from school.

If your son doesn't bring up the incident, broach it at the dinner table. You can say something like this: "Did you hear about . . . ?" and "What did you hear about that?" These questions give you an opportunity to correct any inaccuracies your son may have heard. You can also ask, "What do you think about that?" Your son may or may not give you an answer at that moment. Don't be surprised if he simply grunts or says something like "I don't know" or "I don't care." Boys often believe they must appear tough and invulnerable. You don't have to push your son at that moment, but you may want to revisit the issue later, perhaps when you're alone.

Answer honestly

Share confirmed facts about violent events with your son, without going into gory detail. Be honest about what you *don't* know as well; often, unsupported assumptions and rumors spread quickly in the wake of violence. Point your son toward respected sources of information, including local news sites. Better yet: Consume news stories together.

Empathize when your son asks tough questions like these: "How could this happen?" or "Why would anyone shoot up a school?" Let him know that you, too, have trouble understanding why someone would harm innocent people—and remind him that most people want to protect children.

Don't sugarcoat the facts; your son will find out the truth and when he does, his trust in you will be eroded.

Offer perspective

Wall-to-wall media coverage of violent events may lead tweens to conclude that the world is unsafe. Allow space for your son's feelings, but also share information that provides context. School shootings, for instance, remain statistically rare; most schools and children will never experience a mass shooting. Emphasize the efforts you and others are taking to keep children safe. Talk about his school safety plan.

If your son wants to take action, you have all kinds of options. March for Our Lives, an organization cofounded by survivors of the Parkland, Florida, school shooting, has local chapters in some communities; their website also outlines action steps for students and parents. Futures Without Violence offers a That's Not Cool ambassador program to teach tweens and teens how to spot and derail digital dating abuse, another source of violence.

You can also remind your son that efforts to confront racism, sexism, and systemic inequality help create a more peaceful world. Developing his communication and social-emotional skills and supporting other boys as they share emotions is another way your son can decrease violence, both now and in the future.

Gender and Equality

Girls and women today commonly excel in school, sports, and work. Yet sexism and misogyny linger, and gender equality does not yet exist at home or in the workforce. Women continue to bear the brunt of parenting and household chores, and researchers have found that the sex-based chore gap is present in childhood. According to the Pew Research Center, girls ages 15 to 17 perform about 4.4 hours of housework per week during the school year, while boys the same age only complete an average of 2.8 hours of household chores.

Gender stereotypes and expectations are stubbornly persistent. Your son has probably already noticed that the dads on TV sitcoms tend to be overweight idiots, while the mothers are often thin, young, and beautiful. In video games and movies, macho males are predominant. Boys and girls who step beyond traditional gender roles still face criticism. Author Aaron Gouveia wrote the book *Raising Boys to Be Good Men* in part because his young son was bullied at school for wearing nail polish—an experience that opened Gouveia's eyes to the harms that result from strict gender expectations.

You can help your son question and navigate evolving gender norms. Here's how.

Listen

Your son's perspective and experience of gender and gender expectations will likely be quite different from yours. Listen to him carefully and take his comments seriously. It can be very disturbing for moms to hear their sons say things like "Girls have it made," because mothers are acutely aware of the many challenges women still face. But if your son makes such comments, resist the urge to jump in and point out examples of misogyny and discrimination against women. Instead, dig deeper. Say something like this: "Oh? You think so? Tell me more. How do girls have it made?" Your son's answers will give you insight into his experience and ultimately allow you to add information and correct misconceptions.

As your son gets older, he may become aware of national issues, such as the gender wage gap or the intimidation and sexual harassment of female gamers. When such issues make headlines, talk to your son. Ask him questions like these: "What did you hear about that?" and "What do you think about it?"

Answer honestly

As a woman, you are uniquely positioned to help your son understand gender issues. If your son questions the need for International Women's Day or Day of the Girl Child, you can share specific examples of how you were held back by gender stereotypes. You can also teach him that girls in many parts of the world still do not have access to education. In the same conversation, you should also acknowledge efforts to address boys' concerns. Tell him about International Men's Day, too.

Discuss degrading song lyrics instead of simply telling him to "turn that off!" Explain why words like *bitch* and *ho* are offensive. Call out your son—and his friends—when they insult one another by saying things like "Stop acting like such a girl." Try saying something like this: "What do you mean, 'Stop acting like a girl?'" They'll either flounder for an explanation or say something like "He's so dramatic all the time," which will give you an opportunity to point out that all people feel and express strong emotions at times.

Will your son roll his eyes at you when you have these conversations? Probably. However, it's important to address sexist and misogynistic ideas and language.

Offer perspective

Want to teach boys about gender equality? Model it in your home. Ideally, your son should see men grocery shopping, cooking dinner, cleaning, and doing laundry—and your son should learn to do all the above. He should also see women doing yard work and car maintenance. If you have a male partner, discuss with them the chores your son sees each of you do.

Organizations like Next Gen Men are educating and empowering boys to address gender inequality. Check out their online programming, including moderated digital hangouts where boys can find the support they need to grow into healthy men. The US-based organization A Call to Men offers a free Live Respect curriculum, designed for boys ages 10 to 18, that's been found to significantly increase boys' understanding of gender equity. Ask your son's school or coach to consider implementing the program.

Podcasts like Breaking the Boy Code can help you and your son understand boys' struggles with gender expectations. Consider listening to a few episodes with your son. They're sure to spark discussion.

CONVERSATION STARTERS

→ "How do you feel when someone treats you unfairly? Makes assumptions about you?"

→ "What do you think about 'girl power' T-shirts?"

→ "Why do you think dads are portrayed as doofuses on so many TV shows?"

→ "How do you think we can make the world a safer place for all people?"

Drug Use

Many schools warn kids about the consequences of drug use. But let's be real: Many kids who've sat through these programs can easily recite the dangers of drugs they use anyway.

According to a recent survey by the National Institute on Drug Abuse, 21 percent of eighth graders report having used illicit drugs at some point, and nearly 9 percent have done so within the past month. Marijuana appears to be the substance of choice for most middle school drug users: 15 percent of surveyed eighth graders have tried it and 6.5 percent report using it within the past month.

For many young boys, vaping is their entry to illegal substance use. In 2020, nearly 5 percent of middle schoolers said they used e-cigarettes. Though some middle schoolers who vape only use flavored juice (no nicotine), many unwittingly become hooked on nicotine because they don't realize that most commonly sold products, including Juul cartridges, contain high amounts of nicotine. Kids can also use vape pens to consume marijuana and THC (the active ingredient in marijuana); about 4 percent of eighth graders reported vaping marijuana in 2020.

The reasons for drug use and experimentation are the same as they ever were: Peer pressure. A desire to fit in or look cool. Curiosity. Escape. Self-medication. Research has found that people with unmet mental health needs are more likely to use drugs. Addressing these underlying reasons may be your best bet for keeping your son away from illicit drugs. Build up his self-esteem by giving him ample opportunities to develop his talents. Seek professional help as needed to address symptoms of anxiety, depression, or other mental health challenges. Help your son practice phrases he can use to resist peer pressure: "No way. I think you're just trying to get me in trouble," "Can't—gotta be on top of my game," "You're crazy!"

Alcohol and Underage Drinking

By age 12, approximately one in one hundred children reports using alcohol within the previous month, according to data from the 2018 National Survey on Drug Use and Health. That number increases to one in four by age 17.

The good news is that underage drinking is declining in popularity. Between 2002 and 2018, past-month alcohol use by teens ages 12 to 17 decreased from 18 percent to 9 percent, with the most dramatic declines noted among young males.

Now is the perfect time to discuss alcohol and underage drinking. It can be confusing for children to hear adults talk about avoiding alcohol when they see their parents and others drinking on a regular basis, so be prepared to address that issue head-on. Ideally, you can role-model responsible adult usage—emphasizing why alcohol is only for adults. If you or another family member has a problem with alcohol, seeking professional help is a brave choice that role-models responsibility.

Outline the effects of alcohol, including distorted vision, hearing, and coordination. Most of all, your child needs to know that alcohol can cloud perception, leading to risky decisions. Because tweens (and teens) like to be in control of their lives, painting alcohol as a substance that hijacks their independence may be effective.

Be clear about your family values; evidence has shown that parental disapproval of underage drinking is a major reason kids choose not to drink. Avoid lecturing your son, though. Instead, share information, facts, and values, and listen and respond to your son's questions.

Work and Money

In most states, young people aren't legally eligible for employment until age 14 or 16. However, your son is old enough to learn about the value of money and hard work.

Some families pay children to do chores; others do not. Others pay children for household help that goes beyond their regularly expected chores—paying a moderate amount, for example, to a child who cleans out the garage. Some families give regular allowances, some pay for good grades, and some do none of the above.

Whether you decide to pay your son or not, the tween years are a good time to begin teaching your son money management. Though you may want to protect your son from financial angst, it's a good idea to share some basic information about your family finances. (Most kids are shocked to learn how much food and housing cost!) If you're working extra hours to pay his travel team fees or to save for a family vacation, talk about your efforts and how (and why) your family chooses to prioritize certain expenditures of time and money.

Give your son the opportunity to independently manage some of his money, whether it's from an allowance, gifts, or work. Some families insist that their children divvy up their funds, splitting it between immediate or discretionary spending, long-term savings (toward college tuition, for instance), short-term savings (for desired purchases, such as a video game or a gaming system), and charity. Your son will almost surely make some poor choices with his discretionary spending money and short-term savings, such as spending a lot of money on a cheaply made item or a game that doesn't hold his interest for long. He'll learn from these missteps, though, and gain financial experience that will help him as a young adult.

Instead of simply buying his son football cleats, Benny Nachman gave his son $90—the maximum amount Benny was willing to spend on shoes his son would soon outgrow—and told him to find and purchase a pair of cleats. The boy could keep whatever money was left over.

"He spent the weekend researching cleats," Benny says. In the past, his son usually chose cleats based on style, with little concern for quality or price. Now that the money was "his," the boy carefully weighed quality and price. Ultimately, Nachman's son purchased a $55 pair of cleats, pocketing the $45 difference.

You can try something similar with your own son: Give him a set amount and allow him to buy snacks for the week, a new pair of shoes, or clothes for school. Resist the urge to intervene unless asked. Your son will learn a lot.

Politics

Politics has become a heated topic in the United States and elsewhere, and, as a result, many people are avoiding political discussions with family and friends. You can't—and shouldn't—avoid discussing politics with your son, though. He needs you to help him understand the political process, as well as the issues under discussion.

Don't shy away from hot-button issues, such as abortion and immigration. If your son brings up the topic or you hear a news story while you're in the car together, you can say something like "What do you think about that?" or "What do you know about that?" Such questions will help you ascertain your son's level of understanding, so you can correct misconceptions, fill in information gaps, and add context. Stay calm, no matter what your son says. Kids (boys especially) sometimes say outrageous things simply to see how their parents respond. And tweens often parrot opinions they've heard elsewhere, without fully understanding the issues.

Feel free to share your opinions and beliefs, but don't be surprised or upset if your son disagrees. His views may change many times over the course of the next few years, and your son needs to know that you love him regardless of his political beliefs.

Together, dissect political ads. Your son probably already knows that advertisers use images, colors, and words to convince people to buy products. Remind him that political ads do the same thing. Compare and contrast the phrases and images used to portray the same candidate by their own campaign and the opposition.

Ask your son to share some political memes with you. (If he's active on social media, he's almost certain to encounter them.) Memes tend to oversimplify complex issues, so you can provide additional information, as needed.

Media literacy

Teach your son how to critically evaluate news stories and information. Here's how:

Explain the difference between a fact and an opinion. Facts can be proven with evidence and documentation; an opinion is what someone thinks or believes about something. "It is 0 degrees Fahrenheit outside" is a fact; "It's terrible outside!" is an opinion.

Help your son identify characteristics of reliable sources of information. Information that has been reviewed and verified by experts is more reliable than information that has not been verified. Professional news organizations typically have a fact-checking process; personal blogs and websites do not. News that isn't free tends to be more reliable, so, if you can, purchase a digital subscription for him for a news source you trust.

Show him how to verify information. It's always a good idea to check multiple news sites. You and your son can also use fact-checking websites such as FactCheck and Snopes.

The News Literacy Project offers free online resources to help parents and children build their media literacy skills.

Environmental Concerns and Disasters

Today's tweens are more aware of environmental concerns than previous generations. Even kids who haven't personally experienced a hurricane, wildfire, flood, tornado, or earthquake are acutely aware of the damage inflicted by such environmental disasters. Media mentions of "climate catastrophes" raise awareness of humans' impact on the environment—and trigger anxiety.

According to a 2019 survey by the *Washington Post* and the Kaiser Family Foundation, more than seven in ten teens say climate change will cause a "moderate or great deal of harm" to their generation. You can help your son by acknowledging and discussing environmental concerns. Together, learn more about the environment, climate, and natural disasters; there are tons of excellent documentaries available at your local library and online. (Good ones include *Our Planet, Before the Flood,* and *Chasing Coral.*) Talk to older relatives and others about shifts they've noticed in the weather and seasonal patterns.

Emphasize strategies you and others are taking to keep your child safe. If you live in a wildfire- or hurricane-prone area, for instance, involving your son in your efforts to procure supplies and pack go-bags, should you need to evacuate, may help him feel a bit more in control. You and your son may also choose to become involved in efforts to protect the planet. You can find lots of ideas at earthday.org and projectgivingkids.org.

FOR YOUR REFLECTION

1. On a scale of 0 to 10, how prepared do you feel to discuss these big topics with your son? (0 = not at all; 10 = completely prepared)
2. What steps will you take to bump that number up?
3. Which topic scares you the most? Why?
4. List three resources you'll consult for more information.

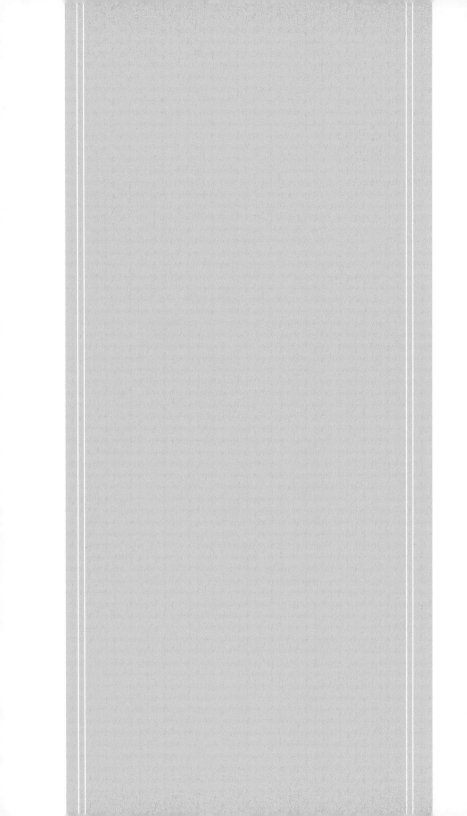

Closing

Mothering a tween boy is an adventure. Sure, there are challenges ahead. Some days, you'll feel like tossing your son out the window. You'll cry and scream and wonder why you ever thought you were up to the task of raising a human being.

But other days, you'll take great pleasure in watching your son mature. You'll look with wonder at his changing face, seeing both the tween before you and the little boy he once was. You'll laugh at his corny jokes and share his excitement as he masters new skills. His bravery may inspire you; together, you may tackle hobbies and activities neither one of you would otherwise consider. (If not for my boys, I guarantee that I would never have jumped off a 20-foot cliff into a lake.)

Keep this book close at hand. Refer to it as needed. Lend it to friends—or buy them their own copies! We can make the world a better place by sharing knowledge that will help boys thrive. Remember:

+ Male puberty may begin sooner than you expect.

+ Boys are more sensitive than you may think.

+ You can't effectively parent your son when you're in a state of stress yourself.

+ Boys need help managing digital distractions and evolving gender norms.

+ Responsible parenting includes an obligation to address family problems, racism, sexism, violence, and inequity.

+ There's no "right way" to raise a boy. You must tailor your parenting to your son and your situation.

When you find yourself doubting your ability to effectively parent your son, reach out to fellow parents of boys. They'll understand your struggles and empathize with your pain and confusion. They may even share a few useful tips.

Above all, love your son, even when he seems unlovable. That's when he needs you the most.

Resources

Books

Codependent No More: How to Stop Controlling Others and Start Caring for Yourself by Melody Beattie

Decoding Boys: The New Science Behind the Subtle Art of Raising Sons by Dr. Cara Natterson

How to Raise a Boy: The Power of Connection to Build Good Men by Michael C. Reichert

The Last Boys Picked: Helping Boys Who Don't Play Sports Survive Bullies and Boyhood by Janet Sasson Edgette and Beth Margolis Rupp

The Last Child in the Woods: Saving Our Children from Nature-Deficit Disorder by Richard Louv

The Mama's Boy Myth: Why Keeping Our Sons Close Makes Them Stronger by Kate Stone Lombardi

Our Wild Calling: How Connecting with Animals Can Transform Our Lives— and Save Theirs by Richard Louv

Raising Boys to Be Good Men: A Parent's Guide to Bringing Up Happy Sons in a World Filled with Toxic Masculinity by Aaron Gouveia

Saving Our Sons: A New Path for Raising Healthy and Resilient Boys by Michael Gurian

Screenwise: Helping Kids Survive (and Thrive) in Their Digital World by Devorah Heitner

To Raise a Boy: Classrooms, Locker Rooms, Bedrooms, and the Hidden Struggles of American Boyhood by Emma Brown

Wild Things: The Art of Nurturing Boys by Stephen James and David S. Thomas

*The Wonder of Boys: What Parents, Mentors and Educators Can Do to Shape Boys into Exceptional Me*n by Michael Gurian

Websites

ADHD Dude (adhddude.com)

AMAZE (amaze.org)

Boys Alive! (boysalive.com)

Broadway Bound Kids (broadwayboundkids.net)

Building Boys (buildingboys.net)

Center for Racial Justice in Education (centerracialjustice.org)

Children of Parents with a Mental Illness (copmi.net.au)

Amy Lang's Birds & Bees & Kids (birdsandbeesandkids.com)

The News Literacy Project (newslit.org)

Organizations

A Call to Men (acalltomen.org)

Futures Without Violence (futureswithoutviolence.org)

March for Our Lives (marchforourlives.com)

Mental Health America (screening.mhanational.org)

Next Gen Men (nextgenmen.ca)

Podcasts

Breaking the Boy Code

ON BOYS parenting podcast

Other

BetterHelp online counseling (betterhelp.com)

Building Boys Bulletin (weekly subscription newsletter: buildingboys .substack.com)

Building Boys Facebook group

K'Bro emotional resiliency app & game (kbro.io)

TalkSpace online counseling (talkspace.com)

References

Chapter 1

Advocates for Youth. 2008. "Growth and Development, Ages Nine to 12—What Parents Need to Know." advocates foryouth.org/resources/health-information/parents-15/#:~: text=PHYSICAL%20DEVELOPMENT,%.

Anthony, Michelle. 2020. "Cognitive Development in 8–10 Year Olds." *Scholastic.* scholastic.com/parents/family-life/creativity-and-critical-thinking /development-milestones/cognitive-development-8-10-year-olds.html.

———. 2020. "The Emotional Lives of 8–10 Year Olds." *Scholastic.* scholastic .com/parents/family-life/social-emotional-learning/development -milestones/emotional-lives-8-10-year-olds.html.

Anzilotti, Amy W. 2020. "What Are Wet Dreams? (For Teens)." *Nemours Teenshealth.* kidshealth.org/en/teens/expert-wet-dreams.html.

APA. 2020. "APA Dictionary of Psychology." dictionary.apa.org /decentration.

Brain Balance. 2020. "Normal Attention Span Expectations by Age." blog.brainbalancecenters.com/normal-attention-span -expectations-by-age.

Brown University. 2020. "The Seven Piagetian Conservation Tasks." cog.brown.edu/courses/cg63/conservation.html.

Centers for Disease Control and Prevention. 2019. "Child Development: Middle Childhood (9–11 Years Old)." cdc.gov /ncbddd/childdevelopment/positiveparenting/middle2.html.

———. 2020. "Data and Statistics on Children's Mental Health." cdc.gov /childrensmentalhealth.

CHOC. 2020. "Growth & Development: 6 to 12 Years (School Age)." choc.org
/primary-care/ages-stages/6-to-12-years.

Downshen, Steven. 2020. "Your Child's Changing Voice (for Parents)."
Nemours KidsHealth. kidshealth.org/en/parents/changing-voice
.html#:~:text=A%20boy's%20voice%2.

Gorney, Cynthia. 2019. "How to Talk to Your Child about Sex Ages 6 to 12."
Consumer Health News | Healthday. consumer.healthday.com/encyclopedia
/children-s-health-10/child-development-news-124/how-to-talk-to-your
-child-about-sex-ages-6-to-12-645918.html#:~:text=Boys%20begin%20.

Gurian, Michael, and Kathy Stevens. 2005. *The Minds of Boys: Saving Our Sons
from Falling Behind in School and Life*. San Francisco: Jossey-Bass.

Hester, Jessica. 2015. "Age-by-Age Advice for Teaching Empathy." *Scholastic.*
scholastic.com/parents/family-life/parent-child/age-age-advice
-teaching-empathy.html.

McAuliffe, Katherine, and Felix Warneken. 2017. "Do Kids Have a Funda-
mental Sense of Fairness?" *Scientific American Blog Network.* blogs
.scientificamerican.com/observations/do-kids-have-a-fundamental
-sense-of-fairness.

Michigan Medicine. 2020. "Egocentric and Magical Thinking."
uofmhealth.org/health-library/te6277.

Natterson, Cara. 2020. *Decoding Boys: New Science behind the Subtle Art of
Raising Sons*. New York: Ballantine Books.

Smith, Craig E., and Felix Warneken. 2016. "Children's Reasoning about
Distributive and Retributive Justice across Development." *Developmental
Psychology* 52 (4): 613–628. doi:10.1037/a0040069.

Walsh, D., and E. Walsh. 2019. "How Children Develop Empathy." *Psychology
Today.* psychologytoday.com/us/blog/smart-parenting-smarter-kids
/201905/how-children-develop-empathy.

Chapter 2

Al-Anon Family Groups. 2020. "Help and Hope for Families and Friends of Alcoholics." al-anon.org.

Bagliere, Joe. 2020. "Science Shows Watching Cute Animals Is Good for Your Health." CNN. cnn.com/2020/09/27/us/watching-cute-animals-study-scn-trnd/index.html.

Beattie, Melody. 1986. *Co-Dependent No More: How to Stop Controlling Others and Start Caring for Yourself.* Center City: Hazelden.

Brown, Joshua, and Joel Wong. 2020. "How Gratitude Changes You and Your Brain." *Greater Good.* greatergood.berkeley.edu/article/item/how_gratitude_changes_you_and_your_brain.

Center for Racial Justice in Education. 2020. "Resources." centerracialjustice.org/resources.

Center for Substance Abuse Treatment. 2004. Treatment Improvement Protocol (TIP) Series, No. 39. ncbi.nlm.nih.gov/books/NBK64258/.

Engelhardt, Jennifer. 2013. "The Developmental Implications of Parentification: Effects on Childhood Attachment." Semantic Scholar. semanticscholar.org/paper/The-Developmental-Implications-of-Parentification-%3A-Engelhardt/48a93aaf7a040112fba80605bdeac1c4905fe2f4.

England, Mary, and Leslie Sim. 2009. "Associations between Depression in Parents and Parenting, Child Health, and Child Psychological Functioning." National Academies Press (US). ncbi.nlm.nih.gov/books/NBK215128.

Harvard Health. 2020. "Giving Thanks Can Make You Happier." Health. harvard.edu/healthbeat/giving-thanks-can-make-you-happier.

Jackson, Kate. 2016. "Children of People with Serious Mental Illness." *Social Work Today* 16 (3): 24. socialworktoday.com/archive/052416p24.shtml.

Julia Cameron Live. 2020. "Morning Pages." juliacameronlive.com
/basic-tools/morning-pages.

Louv, Richard. 2008. *Last Child in the Woods: Saving Our Children from
Nature-Deficit Disorder.* Chapel Hill: Algonquin Books.

Louv, Richard. 2020. *Our Wild Calling: How Connecting with Animals Can Transform Our Lives—and Save Theirs*. Chapel Hill, NC: Algonquin Books.

McMahon, Thomas J., and Suniya S. Luthar. 2007. "Defining Characteristics
and Potential Consequences of Caretaking Burden among Children Living
in Urban Poverty." *American Journal of Orthopsychiatry* 77 (2): 267–281. doi:10
.1037/0002-9432.77.2.267.

Mental Health America. 2020. "Co-Dependency." mhanational.org/issues/
co-dependency.

Nar-Anon Family Groups. 2020. "Nar-Anon Family Groups." nar-anon.org/.

Royal College of Psychiatrists. Accessed March 2021. "Parental Mental
Illness: The Impact on Children and Adolescents: For Parents and
Carers." rcpsych.ac.uk/mental-health/parents-and-young-people
/information-for-parents-and-carers/parental-mental-illness
-the-impact-on-children-and-adolescents-for-parents-and-carers.

Scouting Wire. 2018. "A Scout Is Trustworthy." scoutingwire.org
/a-scout-is-trustworthy/?fbclid=IwAR0FbLCfpQqFswMECXR1ICE
ypeXP6jQCfZX7aTOJhTfFCPKKLcOoOFDkZvE.

Tri-City Medical Center. 2018. "5 Ways the Sun Impacts Your Mental and Physical Health." tricitymed.org/2018/08/5-ways-the-sun-impacts-your
-mental-and-physical-health.

Chapter 3

American Addiction Centers. 2021. "Body Dysmorphia among Male Teenagers and Men: What to Know." americanaddictioncenters.org/male
-eating-disorders/body-dysmorphia.

American Foundation for Suicide Prevention. 2019. "Suicide Statistics."
afsp.org/suicide-statistics.

Anxiety and Depression Association of America. 2021. "Social Anxiety Disorder." adaa.org/understanding-anxiety/social-anxiety-disorder.

Bhojani, Fatima. 2018. "Advice to Parents on Diagnosing and Treating Anxiety Disorders in Young People." Brain & Behavior Research Foundation. bbrfoundation.org/blog/advice-parents-diagnosing-and-treating -anxiety-disorders-young-people#:~:text=Studies%20differ%2C%20 but%20most%20suggest,(10%20to%2020%20percent).

Centers for Disease Control and Prevention. 2019. "Active Listening." cdc. gov/parents/essentials/communication/activelistening.html.

———. 2019. "Death Rates Due to Suicide and Homicide Among Persons Ages 10–24: United States, 2000–2017." cdc.gov/nchs/data/databriefs /db352-h.pdf.

———. 2020. "Data and Statistics on Children's Mental Health." cdc .gov/childrensmentalhealth/data.html.

———. 2021. "Products—Data Briefs—Number 361—March 2020." cdc.gov/ nchs/products/databriefs/db362.htm.

Durlofsky, Paula. 2021. "The Benefits of Emotional Intelligence." *Psych Central.* psychcentral.com/blog/the-benefits-of-emotional -intelligence#1.

Fink, Jennifer. 2018. "Do You Have an ANGRY Boy?" On Boys Podcast. on-boys.blubrry.net/104-anger-and-boys.

———. 2018. "How to Help Boys with Anxiety & Depression." On Boys Podcast. on-boys-podcast.com/125-anxiety-depression-in-boys.

———. 2020. "Suicide Rates Are Rising. Here's What Parents Can Do." *Your Teen Magazine.* yourteenmag.com/health/teenager-mental-health /suicide-rates-are-rising.

Frank, Christina. "Boys and Eating Disorders." Child Mind Institute. childmind.org/article/boys-and-eating-disorders.

Hall, Elizabeth Dorrance. 2018. "Building Emotional Intelligence for Better Relationships." *Psychology Today.* psychology today.com/us/blog/conscious-communication/201806/building -emotional-intelligence-better-relationships.

Lewis, Katherine Reynolds. 2018. *The Good News about Bad Behavior: Why Kids Are Less Disciplined Than Ever—and What to Do about It.* New York City: PublicAffairs.

Lynch, Grace Hwang. 2021. "The Importance of Art in Child Development." PBS. pbs.org/parents/thrive/the-importance-of-art-in-child -development.

Mayo Clinic. 2021. "Social Anxiety Disorder (Social Phobia)—Symptoms and Causes." mayoclinic.org/diseases-conditions/social-anxiety-disorder /symptoms-causes/syc-20353561.

Mental Health America. 2021. "The State of Mental Health in America." mhanational.org/issues/state-mental-health-america.

Mental Health Foundation. 2019. "How Arts Can Help Improve Your Mental Health." mentalhealth.org.uk/blog/how-arts-can-help-improve -your-mental-health#:~:text=The%20arts%20valuable.

On Boys Podcast. 2019. "#Myboycan—This Mom Is Breaking Stereotypes across the Globe!" on-boys-podcast.com/my-boy-can-parenting.

———. 2020. "Boys & Anxiety (W Dr. Mary Wilde)." on-boys.blubrry.net /boys-anxiety-w-dr-mary-wilde.

Pappas, Stephanie. 2019. "APA Issues First-Ever Guidelines for Practice with Men and Boys." *Monitor on Psychology.* apa.org/monitor/2019/01 /ce-corner.

Rosenberg, Jaime. 2021. "Mental Health Issues on the Rise among Adolescents, Young Adults." *AJMC.* ajmc.com/view/mental-health-issues -on-the-rise-among-adolescents-young-adults.

St-Esprit McKivigan, Meg. 2020. "'Nature Deficit Disorder' Is Really a Thing." *New York Times.* nytimes.com/2020/06/23/parenting /nature-health-benefits-coronavirus-outdoors.html.

Teacher Toms Blog. 2020. "Something That Always 'Works.'" teachertom sblog.blogspot.com/2020/11/something-that-always -works.html?fbclid=IwAR0Tv6du3eaF7V6BtDuoKdwGN.

Thomas, Ian. 2016. "Helping Boys Develop Emotional Intelligence." Buildingboys. buildingboys.net/helping-boys-develop -emotional-intelligence/.

Villines, Zawn. 2017. "Study Links School Shootings to Male Gender Role Pressure." Good Therapy. goodtherapy.org /blog/study-links-school-shootings-to-male-gender-role -pressure-1023171.

Waters, Jamie. 2020. "No More Mr Muscle: The Activists Championing Body Confidence For Men." *Guardian.* theguardian .com/lifeandstyle/2020/oct/25/no-more-mr-muscle-the-activists -raising-body-confidence-for-men.

Chapter 4

Anderson, Jill. 2020. "The Benefit of Family Mealtime." Harvard Graduate School of Education. gse.harvard.edu/news/20/04 /harvard-edcast-benefit-family-mealtime#:~:text=Regular%20 family%20dinners%20are%20associated,resilience%20and%20 higher%20self%20esteem.

Dahl, Payal. 2020. "The Shady Side of Ninja." Looper. looper.com/190067/the-shady-side-of-ninja.

Gallegos, Nina. 2021. "Introverted Children 101." Center for Parenting Education. centerforparentingeducation.org/library-of -articles/child-development/introverted-children-101.

Gleason, Tracy R., Sally A. Theran, and Emily M. Newberg. 2017. "Parasocial Interactions and Relationships in Early Adolescence." *Frontiers in Psychology* 8. doi:10.3389/fpsyg.2017.00255.

Harris, Matthew. 2015. "Violence Avoidance: Teaching Boys to Walk Away." Esteem. esteemcommunication.org/violence-avoidance -teaching-boys-to-walk-away/.

Ives, Laurel. 2018. "Boys More 'Cliquey' Than Girls." *BBC News.* bbc.com/news/health-44954170.

Kandell, Ellen. 2019. "Healthy V. Unhealthy Conflict." Alternative Resolutions. alternativeresolutions.net/2019/07/02/healthy-v-unhealthy -conflict.

Katz, Brigit. 2021. "My Child Is a Bully: What Should I Do?" Child Mind Institute. childmind.org/article/what-to-do-if-your-child-is-bullying.

Kelly, Marguerite. 2000. "Breaking Up a Preteen Clique." *Washington Post.* washingtonpost.com/archive/lifestyle/2000/06/07/breaking -up-a-preteen-clique/3ed6652b-11e6-45fd-b4d5-491c2c2c53ce.

Ketteler, Judi. 2018. "Kaboom! Cody! Rudi! Young Flippers Embrace Gtramp, A New Sport for the Instagram Set." *New York Times.* nytimes. com/2018/08/07/well/kaboom-cody-rudi-young-flippers-embrace -gtramp-a-new-sport-for-the-instagram-set.html.

Leonard, Erin. 2018. "Is Your Child in a Toxic Friendship?" *Psychology Today.* psychologytoday.com/us/blog/peaceful-parenting/201807/is-your -child-in-toxic-friendship.

Pacer's National Bullying Prevention Center. 2021. "Bullying Statistics." pacer.org/bullying/info/stats.asp.

Stopbullying.Gov. 2019. "Facts about Bullying." stopbullying.gov /resources/facts.

———. 2019. "Get Help Now." stopbullying.gov/resources/get-help-now.

Chapter 5

ADDitude. 2021. "Test for Dyslexia: Reading Disability Symptoms in Children." additudemag.com/dyslexia-symptoms-test-children.

Autism Speaks. 2021. "Autism Statistics and Facts." autismspeaks.org /autism-statistics.

Berliner, Wendy. 2020. "'Schools Are Killing Curiosity': Why We Need to Stop Telling Children to Shut Up and Learn." *Guardian.* theguardian.com/education/2020/jan/28/schools-killing-curiosity-learn.

Caffrey, Mary. 2021. "Preventing Substance Abuse in ADHD Takes Early Treatment, Harvard Expert Says." *AJMC.* ajmc.com/view /preventing-substance-abuse-in-adhd-takes-early-treatment -harvard-expert-says.

Centers for Disease Control and Prevention. 2020. "Data and Statistics about ADHD." cdc.gov/ncbddd/adhd/data.html.

———. 2020. "Data and Statistics on Autism Spectrum Disorder." cdc.gov /ncbddd/autism/data.html

Common Core State Standards Initiative. 2021. "Grade 7: Introduction." corestandards.org/Math/Content/7/introduction/.

Frye, Devon. 2017. "What Is Dyscalculia? Math Learning Disability Overview." *ADDitude.* additudemag.com/what-is-dyscalculia-overview -and-symptom-breakdown/#:~:text=Dyscalculia%20is%20a%20 math%20learning,%E2%80%9D%20or%20%E2%80%9Cmath%20 dyslexia.%E2%80%9D.

"Girls' and Boys' Performance in PISA." 2020. PISA (Programme for Inter-national Student Assessment) 2018 Results (Volume II). doi:10.1787 /f56f8c26-en.

International Dyslexia Association. 2021. "Dyslexia at a Glance." dyslexiaida .org/dyslexia-at-a-glance.

———. 2021. "Frequently Asked Questions." dyslexiaida.org/frequently -asked-questions-2.

Keilow, Maria, Anders Holm, and Peter Fallesen. 2018. "Medical Treatment of Attention Deficit/Hyperactivity Disorder (ADHD) and Children's Aca-demic Performance." *PLOS ONE* 13 (11): e0207905. doi:10.1371/journal .pone.0207905.

Mayo Clinic. 2021. "Dyslexia—Symptoms and Causes." mayoclinic.org /diseases-conditions/dyslexia/symptoms-causes/syc-20353552.

National Institutes of Mental Health. 2017. "NIMH: Attention-Deficit /Hyperactivity Disorder (ADHD)." nimh.nih.gov/health/statistics /attention-deficit-hyperactivity-disorder-adhd.shtml.

Organisation for Economic Co-operation and Development. 2016. "Gender Gap in Education." oecd.org/gender/data/gender-gap-in-education.htm.

Scheffler, R. M., T. T. Brown, B. D. Fulton, S. P. Hinshaw, P. Levine, and S. Stone. 2009. "Positive Association between Attention-Deficit /Hyperactivity Disorder Medication Use and Academic Achievement during Elementary School." *PEDIATRICS* 123 (5): 1273–1279. doi:10.1542/ peds.2008-1597.

Understood. 2021. "Neurodiversity: What You Need to Know." understood .org/en/friends-feelings/empowering-your-child/building-on-strengths /neurodiversity-what-you-need-to-know.

U.S. Bureau of Labor Statistics. 2020. "College Enrollment and Work Activity of Recent High School and College Graduates Summary." bls.gov/news .release/hsgec.nr0.htm

Workman, Joseph, and Anke Heyder. 2020. "Gender Achievement Gaps: The Role of Social Costs to Trying Hard in High School." *Social Psychology of Education* 23 (6): 1407–1427. doi:10.1007/s11218-020-09588-6.

Chapter 6

American Academy of Dermatology. 2021. "How Often Do Children Need to Take a Bath?" aad.org/public/parents-kids/healthy-habits/parents /bath-often#:~:text=Children%20ages%206%20to%2011,once%20 or%20twice%20a%20week.

Angyal, Chloe. 2017. "Tights, Tutus and 'Relentless' Teasing: Inside Ballet's Bullying Epidemic." *HuffPost*. huffpost.com/entry /ballet-bullying_n_59d5148ce4b0218923e724bf.

Aspen Institute Project Play. 2021. "Youth Sports Facts: Benefits." aspenprojectplay.org/youth-sports-facts/benefits.

Centers for Disease Control and Prevention. 2021. "Do Your Children Get Enough Sleep?" cdc.gov/chronicdisease/resources/infographic /children-sleep.htm.

———. 2021. "Physical Activity Facts: Schools." cdc.gov/healthyschools /physicalactivity/facts.htm.

———. 2021. "School Vending Machines." cdc.gov/healthyschools/nutrition /vending.htm.

———. 2021. "Smart Snacks." cdc.gov/healthyschools/npao/smartsnacks .htm.

De Rosa, Christine J., Kathleen A. Ethier, Deborah H. Kim, William G. Cumberland, Abdelmonem A. Afifi, Jenny Kotlerman, Richard V. Loya, and Peter R.Kerndt. 2010. "Sexual Intercourse and Oral Sex among Public Middle School Students: Prevalence and Correlates." *Guttmacher Institute.* guttmacher.org/journals/psrh/2010/08 /sexual-intercourse-and-oral-sex-among-public-middle -school-students-prevalence.

Donenberg, Geri R., Fred B. Bryant, Erin Emerson, Helen W. Wilson, and Keryn E. Pasch. 2003. "Tracing the Roots of Early Sexual Debut among Adolescents in Psychiatric Care." *Journal of the American Academy of Child & Adolescent Psychiatry* 42 (5): 594–608. doi:10.1097/01 .chi.0000046833.09750.91.

Eat Right. 2018. "Smart Snacks in Schools." eatright.org/food/nutrition /eat-right-at-school/smart-snacks-in-schools.

French, B. H., J. D. Tilghman, and D. A. Malebranche. 2014, March 17. "Sexual Coercion Context and Psychosocial Correlates among Diverse Males." *Psychology of Men & Masculinity.* dx.doi.org/10.1037/a0035915.

Gold, Micheal. 2018. "The ABCs Of L.G.B.T.Q.I.A.+." *New York Times.* nytimes .com/2018/06/21/style/lgbtq-gender-language.html.

Healthychildren.org. 2021. "Masturbation." healthychildren.org/English /ages-stages/gradeschool/puberty/Pages/Masturbation.aspx.

———. 2021. "Protein for the Teen Athlete." healthychildren.org/English /ages-stages/teen/nutrition/Pages/Protein-for-the-Teen-Athlete.aspx.

———. 2021. "A Teenager's Nutritional Needs." healthychildren.org/English /ages-stages/teen/nutrition/Pages/A-Teenagers-Nutritional-Needs.aspx.

———. 2021. "Where We Stand: Vitamins." healthychildren.org/English /healthy-living/nutrition/Pages/Where-We-Stand-Vitamins.aspx.

Intersex Society of North America. 2021. "What Is Intersex?" isna.org/faq /what_is_intersex.

Lewis, Lisa. 2020. "When Teen Boys Use Supplements." *New York Times.* nytimes.com/2020/05/21/well/family/teenage-boys-supplements -protein-creatine.html.

LGBTQIA Resource Center. 2015. "Glossary." lgbtqia.ucdavis.edu/educated /glossary.

Li, Qing. 2006. "Cyberbullying in Schools: A Research of Gender Differences." *School Psychology International.* doi.org/10.1177 /0143034306064547.

Mann, Georgianna, Kathy Hosig, Angang Zhang, Sumin Shen, and Elena Serrano. 2017. "Smart Snacks in School Legislation Does Not Change Self-Reported Snack Food and Beverage Intake of Middle School Students in Rural Appalachian Region." *Journal of Nutrition Education and Behavior* 49 (7): 599-604.e1. doi:10.1016/j.jneb.2017.05.338.

Morales, Christina. 2021. "More Adult Americans Are Identifying as L.G.B.T., Gallup Poll Finds." *New York Times.* nytimes.com/2021/02/24/us /lgbt-identification-usa.html.

Nationwide Children's Hospital. 2021. "Sleep in Adolescents." nationwide-childrens.org/specialties/sleep-disorder-center/sleep-in-adolescents.

Nemours KidsHealth. 2021. "Boys and Puberty." kidshealth.org/en/kids /boys-puberty.html.

———. 2021. "Hygiene Basics." m.kidshealth.org/Nemours/en/teens
/hygiene-basics.html#:~:text=%22oil%20free.%22-,
Sweat%20and%20Body%20Odor,has%20a%20stronger%20
smelling%20odor.

———. 2021. "When Should Kids Start Using Deodorant?" kidshealth
.org/en/parents/deodorant.html#:~:text=As%20kids%20enter%20
puberty%2C%20a,stop%20or%20dry%20up%20perspiration.

———. 2021. "Your Child's Changing Voice." kidshealth.org/en
/parents/changing-voice.html#:~:text=Before%20a%20boy%20
reaches%20puberty,so%20his%20voice%20gets%20deeper.

———. 2021. "Understanding Puberty." kidshealth.org/en/parents
/understanding-puberty.html.

Nemours TeensHealth. 2021. "Becoming a Vegetarian."
kidshealth.org/en/teens/vegetarian.

Newport, Frank. 2018. "In U.S., Estimate of LGBT Population Rises to
4.5%." Gallup. news.gallup.com/poll/234863/estimate-lgbt
-population-rises.aspx.

Orpinas, Pamela. 2015. "The Myth of 'Mean Girls.'" Stopbullying.gov
.stopbullying.gov/blog/2015/09/10/myth-mean-girls.

Risner, Doug. 2014. "Bullying Victimisation and Social Support of
Adolescent Male Dance Students: An Analysis of Findings." *Research in
Dance Education*. doi.org/10.1080/14647893.2014.891847.

Rochman, Bonnie. 2011. "The Results Are In: First National Study
of Teen Masturbation." *TIME*. healthland.time.com/2011/08/11
/boys-masturbate-more-than-girls-seriously.

Suni, Eric. 2021. "How Much Sleep Do Babies and Kids Need?" Sleep Foundation. sleepfoundation.org/children-and-sleep/how-much-sleep
-do-kids-need.

Chapter 7

American Academy of Child and Adolescent Psychiatry. 2015. "Mental Illness in Families." aacap.org/aacap /families_and_youth/facts_for_families/fff-guide/children-of -parents-with-mental-illness-039.aspx.

———. 2018. "Grief and Children." aacap.org/AACAP/Families_and_Youth /Facts_for_Families/FFF-Guide/Children-And-Grief-008.aspx.

American Addiction Centers. 2021. "What Are the Effects of an Alcoholic Father on Children?" americanaddictioncenters.org/alcoholism -treatment/alcoholic-father.

American Psychological Association. 2021. "Children, Youth, Families and Socioeconomic Status." apa.org/pi/ses/resources/publications /children-families.

Arkowitz, Hal, and Scott O. Lilienfeld. 2013. "Is Divorce Bad for Children?" *Scientific American Mind* 24 (1): 68–69. doi:10.1038 /scientificamericanmind0313-68.

Fancher, Michael. 2019. "The Benefits of Shared Custody: Children's Right and Parents' Duty." *Divorce*. divorcemag.com/blog/benefits -of-shared-custody.

Kaplan, Sarah, and Emily Guskin. 2019. "Most American Teens Are Frightened by Climate Change, Poll Finds, and about 1 in 4 Are Taking Action." *Washington Post.* washingtonpost.com/science/most-american-teens -are-frightened-by-climate-change-poll-finds-and-about-1-in-4 -are-taking-action/2019/09/15/1936da1c-d639-11e9-9610-fb56c5522e1c _story.html.

Lipari, Rachel, and Struther L. Van Horn. 2021. "Children Living with Parents Who Have a Substance Use Disorder." Substance Abuse and Mental Health Services Administration. samhsa.gov/data/sites/default/files /report_3223/ShortReport-3223.html.

Rusby, Julie C., John M. Light, Ryann Crowley, and Erika Westling. 2018. "Influence of Parent–Youth Relationship, Parental Monitoring, and Parent Substance Use on Adolescent Substance Use Onset." *Journal of Family Psychology* 32 (3): 310-320. doi:10.1037/fam0000350.

Schuurman, Donna. 2021. "Developmental Grief Responses." Eluna Network. elunanetwork.org/resources/developmental-grief -responses.

Wang, Claire. 2020. "'You Have Chinese Virus!': One in 4 Asian American Youths Experience Racist Bullying, Report Says." *NBC News*. nbcnews.com/news/asian-america/25-percent-asian -american-youths-racist-bullying-n1240380.

Yale Medicine. 2021. "Parental Depression: How It Affects a Child." yalemedicine.org/conditions/how-parental-depression-affects-child.

Zhu, Yannan, Xu Chen, Hui Zhao, Menglu Chen, Yanqiu Tian, Chao Liu, Zhuo Rachel Han, Zhuo Rachel et al. 2019. "Socioeconomic Status Disparities Affect Children's Anxiety and Stress-Sensitive Cortisol Awakening Response through Parental Anxiety." *Psychoneuroendocrinology* 103: 96–103. doi:10.1016/j.psyneuen.2019.01.008.

Chapter 8

Carroll, Rory. 2016. "'You Were Born in a Taco Bell': Trump's Rhetoric Fuels School Bullies Across US." *Guardian*. theguardian.com /us-news/2016/jun/09/california-primary-trump-rhetoric-school-bully.

Child Trends. 2021. "Children's Exposure to Violence." childtrends.org /indicators/childrens-exposure-to-violence.

de León, Concepción. 2019. "Jason Reynolds Is on a Mission." *New York Times.* nytimes.com/2019/10/28/books/jason-reynolds-look-both -ways.html.

Edwards-Levy, Ariel. 2018. "In 1968, Nearly a Third of Americans Said MLK Brought His Assassination on Himself." *HuffPost.* huffpost.com /entry/in-1968-nearly-a-third-of-americans-said-mlk-brought-his-killing -on-himself_n_5ac51373e4b0aacd15b7d37b.

Gross, Natalie. 2016. "Schools Offer Counseling As Many Latino Students Face Bullying, Uncertainty after Trump Win—Education Writers Association." Education Writers Association. ewa.org /blog-latino-ed-beat/schools-offer-counseling-many-latino -students-face-bullying-uncertainty-after.

Healthychildren.Org. 2021. "Childhood Exposure to Violence." healthychildren.org/English/safety-prevention/at-home/Pages /Crime-Violence-and-Your-Child.aspx.

Johnson, Annysa. 2018. "Federal Investigation Found 100-plus Examples of Racial Disparities in MPS Suspensions." *Milwaukee Journal Sentinel.* jsonline.com/story/news/education/2018/03/29/federal-probe-found -100-plus-examples-racial-disparities-mps-suspensions/463464002.

Lazareck, Samuel, Jennifer A. Robinson, Rosa M. Crum, Ramin Mojtabai, Jitender Sareen, and James M. Bolton. 2012. "A Longitudinal Investigation of the Role of Self-Medication in the Development of Comorbid Mood and Drug Use Disorders." *Journal of Clinical Psychiatry* 73 (05): e588–e593. doi:10.4088/jcp.11m07345.

Lewis, Daniel. 2020. "Larry Kramer, Playwright and Outspoken AIDS Activist, Dies at 84." *New York Times.* nytimes.com/2020/05/27/us /larry-kramer-dead.html.

National Institute of Justice. 2016. "Children Exposed to Violence." nij.ojp. gov/topics/articles/children-exposed-violence#:~:text=%5B1%5D%20 Exposure%20to%20violence%20can,in%20criminal%20behavior%20 as%20adults.

National Institute on Drug Abuse. 2020. "Monitoring the Future Study: Trends in Prevalence of Various Drugs." drugabuse.gov/drug-topics /trends-statistics/monitoring-future/monitoring-future-study -trends-in-prevalence-various-drugs.

Pinsker, Joe. 2021. "The Myth That Gets Men Out of Doing Chores."
   The Atlantic. theatlantic.com/family/archive/2021/01/boys-men
   -messy-chores/617845.

Ritschel, Chelsea. 2020. "Check Your Privilege: What Is the Trend Going
   Viral on TikTok?" *The Independent.* independent.co.uk/life-style
   /check-your-privilege-tiktok-white-privilege-kenya-big-mamma
   -racism-a9547731.html.

Trent, Maria, Danielle G. Dooley, and Jacqueline Dougé. 2019. "The Impact
   of Racism on Child and Adolescent Health." *Pediatrics* 144 (2): e20191765.
   doi:10.1542/peds.2019-1765.

Truth Initiative. 2021. "E-Cigarettes: Facts, Stats and Regulations."
   truthinitiative.org/research-resources/emerging-tobacco
   -products/e-cigarettes-facts-stats-and-regulations#:~:
   text=In%202020%2C%2082.9%25%20of%20youth,middle%
   20school%20users%20(400%2C000).

U.S. Government Accountability Office. 2018. "K-12 Education: Discipline
   Disparities for Black Students, Boys, and Students with Disabilities."
   gao.gov/products/GAO-18-258.

Wang, Teresa W., Linda J. Neff, Eunice Park-Lee, Chunfeng Ren,
   Karen A. Cullen, and Brian A. King. 2020. "E-Cigarette Use among
   Middle and High School Students—United States, 2020." *Morbidity and
   Mortality Weekly Report* 69 (37): 1310–1312. doi:10.15585/mmwr.mm6937e1.

Worldhealth.net. 2021. "Gender Differences in the Epidemiology of Alcohol
   Use and Related Harms in the United States." worldhealth.net/news
   /gender-differences-epidemiology-alcohol-use-and-related-harms
   -united-states.

Index

Acknowledgments

This book would not exist if not for my four boys. My career would not exist, but for my boys. *I* would not be the person I am today, if not for my boys. They survived my mistakes and showed me, through example, the importance of pursuing my passions in the world. They opened my eyes to boys' experiences in the world and I am forever grateful.

My husband, Mike Tennessen, provided logistical support and emotional encouragement as I wrote this book. He cooked so that I could keep writing. He set up a desk and bought a second office chair and understood completely when I spent hours of our weekends hunched over a keyboard. His unwavering belief in me gives me strength.

Catherine Miller assisted me with research, combing through file after file so that I could focus on writing. I could not have written this book in three months—while maintaining my freelance career—without her help.

About the Author

 **Jennifer L.W. Fink** is the creator of BuildingBoys .net and cohost of the podcast *On Boys: Real Talk about Parenting, Teaching & Reaching Tomorrow's Men*. She's a freelance journalist whose writing has been published by the *New York Times*, the *Washington Post, U.S. News and World Report*, FOX News, *Parents*, and *Parade*. Fink is the mother of four sons, and a long-time member of the American Society of Journalists and Authors (ASJA). She is currently working on her second book about raising boys.

CPSIA information can be obtained
at www.ICGtesting.com
Printed in the USA
JSHW010811170621
15967JS00005BA/51